THE LIFE AND TIMES OF WILLIAM HENRY HARRISON

SAMUEL JONES BURR

Published by Left of Brain Books

Copyright © 2021 Left of Brain Books

ISBN 978-1-396-32182-5

First Edition

All rights reserved. No part of this publication may be reproduced, distributed, or transmitted in any form or by any means, including photocopying, recording, or other electronic or mechanical methods, without the prior written permission of the publisher, except in the case of brief quotations embodied in critical reviews and certain other noncommercial uses permitted by copyright law. Left of Brain Books is a division of Left of Brain Onboarding Pty Ltd.

Table of Contents

PREFACE.	1
CHAPTER I.	2
CHAPTER II.	6
CHAPTER III.	11
CHAPTER IV.	15
CHAPTER V.	19
CHAPTER VI.	23
CHAPTER VII.	29
CHAPTER VIII.	33
CHAPTER IX.	37
CHAPTER X.	42
CHAPTER XI.	46
CHAPTER XII.	51
CHAPTER XIII.	56
CHAPTER XIV.	61
CHAPTER XV.	66
CHAPTER XVI.	71
CHAPTER XVII.	77
CHAPTER XVIII.	82
CHAPTER XIX.	88
CHAPTER XX.	94
CHAPTER XXI.	101
CHAPTER XXII.	105
CHAPTER XXIII.	110
CHAPTER XXIV.	114

CHAPTER XXV.	118
CHAPTER XXVI.	123
CHAPTER XXVII.	127
CHAPTER XXVIII.	131
CHAPTER XXIX.	136
APPENDIX.	139
Correspondence between General Wayne and Major Campbell.	139
Mischecanocquah to Governor Harrison.	143
Mr. Eustis to General Harrison.	144
Colonel Johnson to General Harrison.	145
The Officers of the Army to the Public.	146
Major Croghan's Card.	148
Indiana Legislature and Gen. Harrison.	150
Reply of General Harrison.	151
General Harrison to General Bolivar.	153
General Harrison to Hon. Harmar Denny.	165
General Harrison to the Editor of the Ohio Confederate.	167

PREFACE.

In presenting the "Life and Times of WILLIAM HENRY HARRISON" to the public, some explanation of the title may be necessary. We have christened our work *Life and Times*, to distinguish it from several other books already out upon the same subject. By "Times," we do not mean all the events of the country during the life of HARRISON, but merely those with which he was immediately connected.

In recording these, we have been governed solely by facts, and we leave these facts to speak for themselves. If he were not at this moment before the people for their suffrages as a candidate for a great and important station, we might have indulged in compliment and praise; but we have no disposition, and disclaim all intention of making our history political.

In our Appendix will be found many papers of great interest, connected with the life of General HARRISON, and to which we invite attention.

In preparing our work for publication, we have been greatly assisted by Butler's "History of Kentucky"; McAffee's "History of the Late War"; Hall's "Life of Harrison", and Dawson's "Life of Harrison". We have also used freely the Washington Mirror; Niles' Register; the Congressional Journals, and the Journals of the Legislatures of Ohio, Indiana, &c.

We return our acknowledgments to several gentlemen who have kindly furnished us with much important information, among whom we must particularize, General LESLIE COMBS, of Lexington, Kentucky, and our talented fellow-citizen, RUFUS DAWES, Esq. To the latter, we are very largely indebted.

CHAPTER I.

Birth, Parentage, and Education of William Henry Harrison.
His First Appointment by Washington.

IN the most strict sense of the word, every man *belongs* to his country, and the lives of all who have distinguished themselves, whether in the field or in the forum, should be carefully recorded, and their acts minutely and faithfully engrossed; as lessons of instruction and examples for emulation to after generations. Under a republic, offices of trust, honor, and emolument, are open to all, and he who served his country in any manner whatever, retires from that service into private life, and mingles once more with those, who, for a short time, honored him with power. However worthy his deeds, no title of nobility follows him into his retirement; no privileged designation of mere sound descends to his son and his son's son. The child may look back with conscious pride, to the whole life of his father, but he must still depend upon his own exertions, his own acts, and his own genius, for any distinction shown to himself. It is one of the greatest blessings of our form of government, that we are not honored because our fathers were. Were it otherwise, how many silly coxcombs would be bend to, merely because their fathers were great men? "Every man for himself," is a true Yankee motto, and should be that of every free people. This saying is quite common, and is often perverted, but we apply it only in all honorable enterprize, and where ambition is governed solely by a desire for the general weal.

Yet, when a man can proudly refer to the achievements of his fathers, it stimulates his mind to be worthy of such a parentage, and urges him to attempt a career as bright and glorious as that of his ancestry. There are few of our countrymen who can make such a retrospect with as much pleasure as the subject of our present memoir, General WILLIAM HENRY HARRISON.

Descended from a long line of patriots, he would have proved recreant to the best blood in America, had he been less than they. Thrown early into public life by the requirement of a young and struggling country, his opportunities gave scope to his superior intellect, and step by step he rose in the estimation of the people, gathering fresh laurels at each advance, until there is barely room enough for another glorious chaplet upon his noble brow.

WILLIAM HENRY HARRISON, was born on the 9th day of February, 1773, at a place called Berkley, on the James River, about 25 miles below Richmond, in Charles City County, in the State of Virginia. He is a lineal descendant of that General Harrison, who bore a prominent part in the English civil wars, and who held an important command in the armies of the Commonwealth.

BENJAMIN HARRISON, the father of William Henry, was a delegate to the Continental Congress, in 1774–5–6. It was between him and John Hancock, that the amicable contention took place respecting the Presidency of the Congress. Peyton Randolph, and Benjamin Harrison, were brothers-in-law, and upon the decease of the former, who was first President of Congress, it was the wish of the Southern members that Mr. Harrison should be selected to fill the chair vacated by the death of his relative. He was fully informed of the various sectional prejudices existing at that momentous crisis, and exerted all his influence in favor of his friendly rival, JOHN HANCOCK. He reasoned with his colleagues upon the importance of conciliating the Northern feeling, and succeeded in obtaining for the Massachussetts member a unanimous vote.

WALN, in his Biography of the Signers of the Declaration of Independence, says of Mr. Hancock:—

"With a modesty not unnatural of his years, and a consciousness of the difficulty he might experience in filling a station of such high importance and responsibility, he hesitated to take the seat. Mr. Harrison was standing beside him, and with the ready good humour that he loved a joke, even in the Senate House, he seized the modest candidate in his athletic arms, and placed him in the presidential chair; then turning to some of the members around, he exclaimed, 'We will show mother Britain how little we care for her, by making a Massachussetts man our president, whom she has excluded from pardon by public proclamation.'"

BENJAMIN HARRISON, afterward filled the executive chair of Virginia, at a time when the energies of the bold, prompt, and daring, were requisite to inspire his countrymen. With the example of such a father, WILLIAM HENRY HARRISON would have been less than man had he not been brave and patriotic. His father was a patriot of the noblest class when it was death to be so known. He made his opinions public, with the gallows staring him in the face, and fled not from the enemy who watched, but to slay. When destruction hung over his country, he was by the side of his daring companions to breast and share with them the ruthless storm.

When the sacred Declaration of Independence was passed, he joined the fathers of the Union, and signed that famous document. It was a solemn hour, and not a man placed his name to that paper, who did not expect desolation and death to wait upon the deed. So well convinced were all of imminent risk of the act, that when Charles Carroll signed, remark was made, "There go millions," the some one added, "but as there are many of the name he may escape by its not being known positively which it is." "Not so," replied the signer, and immediately added "of Carrollton." Hence it is that this name is accompanied with his place of residence.

Though well aware of the enormous danger incurred, not a man wavered in his purpose. When they pledged "our lives and fortunes, and our sacred honors," they knew the penalty, yet not a soul trembled for the consequences.

WILLIAM HENRY HARRISON was the third and youngest son, and though the father was poor in this world's goods, the son received a rich and noble inheritance—the legacy of a name surrounded by glorious achievements and connected with the first struggles of his country for freedom. To a soul filled with honor and burning to imitate the noble example, such legacy was all he asked—all he required.

Young Harrison was educated at Hampden, Sydney College, and afterward applied himself diligently to the study of medicine. In his boyhood he had wished for some opportunity to serve his country, for he

> "—— had heard of battles, and longed
> To follow to the field some warlike lord."

He was about to graduate as a physician, when fresh reports of the daring deeds of his countrymen in the western wilds; tales of midnight murders in the new settlements, roused again the lambent desire to share the perils of his fellow-citizens and he resolved to join the frontier army;—not to spread plasters and sew up gashes, but as a soldier of liberty.

His guardian was the celebrated ROBERT MORRIS, who so frequently relieved the Continental army from his private fortune, and was the intimate friend of the immortal WASHINGTON. Perceiving in young Harrison the germ of true greatness, Mr. Morris endeavored to persuade him from his purpose until he had the advantage of every scientific acquirement within reach, and it was supposed that the kindness of his nature and gentleness of manner, had fitted him peculiarly for the profession which he had first adopted.

The army then serving in the west under General ST. CLAIR, had been raised for the express purpose of preventing the repeated outrages and barbarities committed by the Indians, and the young student resolved to join this little baud and serve his country where she most needed the gallantry of her sons.

The opposition of his excellent guardian was not sufficient to deter him from his purpose, and as his design was approved by WASHINGTON, who had also been the warm friend of his father, he received from that noble warrior an ensign's commission in the first regiment of United States Artillery, then stationed at Fort Washington.

Here commenced the public life of Harrison, and long, active, and eventful has it been. Here under a daring and experienced soldier, the young officer began his glorious career. At the early age of nineteen he adopted the service of his country as his profession, and not contented with his uniform merely to exhibit it in the streets of a city, he repaired immediately to a dangerous position, to give the strength of his boyish arm to defend a frontier which may be said at that time, almost to have been in the possession of a ruthless, cruel, and vindictive foe.

We cannot close this chapter without drawing a comparison between our boy soldier and LAFAYETTE. The latter left his own country to aid a struggling people in obtaining and maintaining their freedom. The former relinquished a peaceful profession in which his talents would soon have rendered him independent, to share the dangers of a wilderness—the exposure to a cold and changeable climate, and the tomahawks and scalping knives of a sculking midnight foe; and all this to assist men expecting night after night to be butchered in their sleep. Both heroes entered upon their arduous profession at nearly the same period of life—both triumphed, and both lived long to benefit mankind by their dazzling genius, their warlike enterprise and their profound counsel.

CHAPTER II.

The Indian war—Hostile tribes—Defeat of Harmer—Organization of a new army under St. Clair—Advance of the same—St. Clair's defeat—State of the country—Parties in Congress—Foreign influence.

IN 1783 peace was concluded between Great Britain and the United States of America, yet our country was still the scene of war and bloodshed. During the revolutionary contest, most of the Indian tribes upon the frontier had been induced to take up arms in favor of Great Britain, and they now refused to lay down the hatchet, determined still to continue their murders until the people of the United States should be driven from the western settlements.

A few of the tribes entered into treaties of peace with this country, but those north and west of the Ohio persisted in maintaining their barbarous and devastating hostility. The incursions of the latter were principally directed against the people of west Pennsylvania, and a few settlements which had been formed in the Northwestern Territory, or that portion of it which is now the state of Ohio.

There were seven tribes at this time, who refused altogether to enter into a peace, and who persisted in their midnight murders upon the border. The principal of these were the MIAMIES, who occupied all of Indiana, a large part of Illinois, and a good tract of country west of the Scioto, in Ohio. They were a brave and warlike people, but extremely obstinate. They hearkened but little even to their own chiefs, so that it can scarcely be supposed but they would be among the very last to abandon a war, to which they were daily urged by Englishmen, and while too, they could be supplied with guns and ammunition from the British forts.

The HURONS occupied the southern shore of Lake Erie, and a more desperate set of dogs were not to be found through the whole region of the west. Again and again would they rally when driven back, and rarely was it that they abandoned the pursuit of a foe. The HURONS or WYANDOTS have been known to follow a beaten and retreating enemy for more than a week, and never rose the sun during the whole time, but his beams were darkened with the blood of mothers and babes.

The DELAWARES having been driven from their beautiful flat-lands by the white settler, left COAQUANAC[1] for the west, and gradually retired, until we find them, at the time of which we write, dwelling within the present limits of Ohio.

This tribe had but little to complain of compared with many others. The land owned by the DELAWARES, or LENI LENAPES, had, to a great extent, been purchased and paid for.

In the north of Ohio were the SHAWNEES, who had made their way from the extreme south, and are supposed to have been driven by some stronger tribe, from Georgia or Florida.

On the peninsula of Michigan were the CHIPPEWAS, the OTTOWAS, and the POTOWATOMIES. All these tribes, and some of them were at that time very large and numbered many thousands of warriors, were engaged in desperate contests with the whites, for the purpose of stopping forever the emigration of the early settlers to the west.

"My mind and heart are upon that river," pointing to the Ohio, "may that river ever continue to run, and remain the boundary of lasting peace between the Americans, and the Indians on its opposite shore."

This was the toast given by CORNPLANTER at the table of Gen. WAYNE, in March, 1793. We step a little in advance of our history to bring in this sentiment of a friendly chief, that our renders may be able to judge of the feeling at that time existing among the Indians, towards the white settlers. Assassination was the deed of every night, and though our revolutionary war closed in 1783, yet the Indians still committed their outrages, and were often assisted by the English; who, though they did not as a nation war upon us, yet they had their men and officers mingled with and directing the hostile tribes.

Mr. Hall in noticing this subject, says:—

"From 1783 to 1790, it was estimated that 1500 men, women and children, had been killed or taken prisoners by the Indian upon the waters of the Ohio; more than 2000 horses were stolen from the inhabitants; houses had been burned, fields ravaged, boats plundered, and property destroyed, to an

---

[1] The Indian name of Philadelphia.

unknown amount. Still the settlements grew, and the gallant pioneers sustained the war with undaunted spirit. The British, in defiance of a solemn treaty, continued to hold military posts within our acknowledged territory, to tamper with the tribes in our limits, and faithlessly to supply the munitions of war, to be used against a civilized people at peace with herself."

The defeat of Brigadier General HARMER, a brave and skilful officer, and the total destruction of his gallant army, by hordes of savages, filled the whole frontier with apprehension and despair, whilst it inspired the Indians with renewed confidence; and flushed with victory, they extended their barbarities from town to town, and house to house, with the apparent determination to annihilate every settler on the border.

The inhabitants of the frontier called for a new army, which was raised and placed under the command of Major General ST. CLAIR, a veteran of the revolution, who possessed the entire confidence of WASHINGTON. It was necessary that the arms of America should triumph over all her foes, whether foreign or domestic, that the country might be secure from rapine, murder and devastation, and that the young nation should be respected by the whole world.

The new army marched to the seat of war, and the venerable commander exerted all his skill for the success of his hardy soldiers; but unfortunate events occurred which were wholly unexpected, and the meritorious efforts of ST. CLAIR, in behalf of his country, were only attended with defeat and destruction.

The army advanced slowly and cautiously toward the head waters of the Wabash, opening a road, and building forts at suitable distances. By the first of November, 1791, ST. CLAIR found himself in the midst of the Indian country, and within fifteen miles of the Miami villages. On the 4th, about daylight, his camp was suddenly attacked by an immense body of savages, lead on by MESHECUNNAQUA, or the LITTLE TURTLE, a distinguished chief and great warrior of the Miamies, and Buckongehelas, first chief of the Delawares, aided by white auxiliaries from Canada.

The assailants were well protected by the shelter of the trees and the frequent mounds of earth. They fired from the ground and were scarcely to be seen, except when they rose to spring from one shelter to another. They advanced rapidly in front, and upon either flank, up to the very mouths of the American field pieces.

The militia occupying the front were dismayed by the impetuosity and violence of this unexpected attack, and falling back upon the regulars, threw them into confusion. In vain the officers endeavoured to rally and re-form their men; their success was only partial. Twice were the Indians driven back by desperate charges, but while they gave way at one point to the bayonets of our soldiers, from every other quarter they poured in a heavy and destructive fire upon the lines, until the whole army was thrown into the greatest confusion, and a most disorderly retreat ensued.

For several miles the Indians pursued their conquered foe, and the woods were literally strewed with the bleeding bodies of the dead and dying. The camp was completely deserted, and was afterward plundered by the victors.

The army suffered most cruelly. Of fourteen hundred men engaged, five hundred and thirty were killed, and three hundred and sixty wounded. Many of the latter died within a few days after the battle. Thirty officers were slain, and among them General BUTLER, a distinguished soldier of the revolutionary struggle.

A series of terrible disasters had already rendered the war unpopular, and this last defeat filled the whole country with distress, mourning, and apprehension. The implacable foe had gained success upon success, until, flushed with victory, he ventured still closer to the encampments and threatened to attack settlements still further east. The bleeding scalp, torn from the struggling and wounded victim, was flouted in the face of the American soldiery, and every species of insult offered to their dead and dying companions.

So great was the consternation spread throughout the country, that even the brave and daring shrunk from a contest fruitful only in labour, disaster, and defeat. Victory over such an enemy would bring but little glory; and if conquered, excruciating tortures and horrid deaths were certain to await the vanquished.

Parties for and against the further prosecution of the war were forming through the land, and the two fatal expeditions had drained the treasury, and drawn largely from the resources of the country. In Congress parties pro and con also existed, and all the energy, coolness, and discrimination of the mighty intellect of our great Washington were required to crush the discontented factions, and to secure the permanency of those glorious institutions which had been established by seven years of toil, and the outpouring of oceans of patriotic blood.

Had the war at that moment been given over, it is highly probable that England would have thrown her forces openly into the western wilderness, and commenced another trial to reduce the free states. Though she could never have gained *this* object, she might have possessed herself of an immense territory at the north-west, and retarded for many years the developement of the blessings of freedom, and the proof of that which was then considered a mere assertion—"That man is capable of self-government."

CHAPTER III.

British Influence—General Wayne appointed to the command of the Legion of the United States—Desertion—Discipline and State of the New Army.

THE war with the north-western tribes was no longer a local matter, but had gradually risen in importance, until it became a national contest, jeoparding the free institutions of our new country. In the movements of the foe was seen the directing influence of a more experienced hand, and although GREAT BRITAIN had abandoned as a government, efforts to recover the colonies, yet it was too clearly perceived that she did not restrain her subjects from co-operating with, aiding, advising, and leading the hostile bands of Indians.

At his first interview with Mr. ADAMS, the KING of ENGLAND expressed the following sentiment:—

"I was the last to conform to the separation; but the separation having been made, I would be the first to meet the friendship of the United States as an independent power."

The people did not join with their sovereign in this declaration, but continued to throw every obstacle that could be thought of in the way of the rising Republic.

The frequent defeats rendered it imperative that the army should be placed under the command of a military chief of well earned reputation; a cautious, discreet, brave, and energetic soldier. The two most prominent at that period, were GEORGE ROGERS CLARK and ANTHONY WAYNE. They had both fought in the revolution; held separate commands, and had planned and executed the most daring and successful enterprizes. The latter was known through the whole army, and in every quarter of the Union, as MAD ANTHONY, from his eventful fortunes and daring adventures. The calculating mind of the discriminating WASHINGTON singled out MAD ANTHONY, to command the western army, and he at once received orders to that effect.

Brigadier Generals JAMES WILKINSON and THOMAS POSEY, distinguished revolutionary officers, were associated with General WAYNE.

In the *Casket* of 1830, published by Mr. Atkinson, in Philadelphia, we find an article upon the subject of the frontier war, written evidently by a person intimately acquainted with the subject. We copy below his account of the formation of WAYNE's Legion, or "The Legion of the United States," by which name it was designated and known.

"On the 25th of May, 1792, General WAYNE having been furnished by the Secretary of War with the instructions of the President, in which it was emphatically expressed, *that another defeat would be inexpressibly ruinous to the reputation of the government,* took leave of his family and friends, and repaired to Pittsburgh, the place appointed for the rendezvous of the troops, and where he arrived in June. By the new organization, the army was to consist of one Major General, four Brigadier Generals, and their respective staffs; the commissioned officers, and five thousand one hundred and twenty non-commissioned officers and privates—the whole to be denominated '*The Legion of the United States.*' The legion to be divided into four sub-legions, each to consist of commissioned officers named, and one thousand two hundred and eighty non-commissioned officers and privates. The previous army having been nearly annihilated, a new one was to be recruited. Most of the experienced officers having been slain in the defeats of HARMER and ST. CLAIR, or resigned their commissions, the labors of the commanding general were augmented to an extent which nothing but the most unwearied patience and ardent zeal could have performed. Many of the officers, as well as of the soldiers, had yet to learn the rudiments of the profession. The organization of the troops, military tactics, discipline, &c., devolved so far upon the General, as to leave him scarcely time, without infinite labor, to keep up the correspondence incident to his station. His efforts were indefatigable, and it is impossible at the present day to form an adequate idea of the difficulties he had to encounter; the labors to perform, and the obstacles to surmount. So panic-struck was the whole country at the repeated and bloody successes of the enemy, that an engagement with them was looked to as certain defeat. A perfect horror seemed to seize the recruits, when marched from the rendezvous where they had enlisted, and their faces turned to join the enemy. In a letter to the Secretary of War, dated Pittsburgh, 20th July, 1792, General

WAYNE says, 'The detachment under Major ASHTON arrived at this place on Monday; Lieutenant CAMPBELL's with STOKES' dragoons, and Captain FAULKNER's riflemen, on Tuesday, I am, however, sorry to inform you of the alarming desertion that prevailed in ASHTON's detachment, and STOKES' dragoons. Not less than fifty of the former, and seven of the latter deserted on their march between Carlysle and Pittsburgh.'

"Another fact will show the degree of terror that the name of Indian had inspired, and the extraordinary difficulties the general had to surmount, to introduce obedience, self-confidence, and courage. A letter to the Secretary of War, dated Pittsburgh, 10th of August, 1792, says, 'Desertions have been frequent and alarming. Two nights since, upon a report that a large body of Indians were close in our front, I ordered the troops to form for action, and rode along the line to inspire them with confidence, and gave a charge to those in the redoubts which I had recently thrown up in our front, and on the right flank, to maintain their posts at any expense of blood, until I could gain the enemy's rear with the dragoons; but such was the defect of the human heart, that from excess of cowardice, one-third of the sentries deserted from their stations, so as to leave the most accessible places unguarded.'

"By the salutary measures adopted to introduce order and discipline, the army soon began to assume its proper character. The troops were daily exercised in all the evolutions necessary to render them efficient soldiers, and more especially in those manœuvers proper in a campaign against savages. Firing at a mark was constantly practised, and rewards given to the best marksmen. To inspire emulation, the riflemen and infantry strove to excel, and the men soon attained to an accuracy that gave them confidence in their own prowess. On the artillery the general impressed the importance of that arm of the service. The dragoons he taught to rely on the broadsword, as all important to victory. The riflemen were made to see how much success must depend on their coolness, quick, and accuracy; while the infantry were led to place entire confidence in the bayonet, as the certain and irresistible weapon, before which savages could not stand. The men were instructed to charge in open order; and each to rely on himself, and to prepare for a personal contest with the enemy. The confidence inspired, and the rapid improvement in discipline, are frequently mentioned with pleasure in the letters of the Commanding General, written during the autumn; but the season was too far advanced before a reasonable force could be collected to warrant active operations.

Such was the situation of the country—such the position of the army, and such the foe to be encountered at the time Ensign HARRISON joined his regiment at Fort Washington, which stood upon the site of the present beautiful city of Cincinnati, in Ohio. It was no holiday parade—no marching and counter-marching where none but friends are seen; but it was active service against an implacable assassin who stole upon his victim in the still hour of night, and murdered him as he slept unconscious of his danger. A majority of those the young Ensign associated with, were like himself, raw recruits, and it was necessary to have constant drills for the purpose of instructing the soldiers and giving them confidence in themselves. The command wad wisely placed by WASHINGTON in the hands of MAD ANTHONY, and the latter kept his men continually at work.

The author was speaking but a few days since with a veteran who served under General WAYNE during the whole time he was in the west. In speaking of the daily exercises imposed upon the army, he saith, "Indeed, sir, the general kept us busy. We had a regular school of it, morning, noon and night, and Wayne didn't give over till he thought we knew near about as much as he did. When he had to stop a bit, for, you know, it would not do for the soldiers to know more than their leader. The practising was all the time, and faith, sir, we weren't allowed to whisper in school, and hang the play we could take out of it, for you see there were no *between times*."

The few last words probably give the best idea that we could possibly have of MAD ANTHONY's character, and at the same time form as handsome a compliment as could be paid him as a soldier. With him there were no "between times," he was constantly upon the alert, and always at his post.

CHAPTER IV.

Ensign Harrison reaches Fort Washington—Habits of the soldiers—Harrison's temperance—His first service—Gains the applause of St. Clair—Is promoted to a lieutenancy—Wayne's position at Legionville—The Legion proceeds to Fort Washington, where it is joined by Lieutenant Harrison.

ENSIGN Harrison reached Fort Washington directly after the defeat of General ST. CLAIR, which we have already recorded. He arrived in time to witness the gathering in of the vanquished and disheartened troops at that post. But a short time before they had marched out in all the pride of conscious strength. They now returned, such of them as lived to return—a mutilated, spirit-broken, and disorganized body. Squads came flying before the enemy who yet lurked in their rear to goad and lash and torture the conquered victim.

The savage foe exulting in recent victory ventured almost to the very gates of the fort, and closely watched for another opportunity to glut upon the blood of the soldiery, the whole defence of the border was in the hands of a few, and they having nothing to look back upon but disaster and defeat. It was scarcely to be wondered at, that under these circumstances the way-worn soldier flew to his bottle for forgetfulness, and sought in other vices means to dispel the gloom that hung over his hopes. Intemperance and debauchery crept insensibly upon the officers as well as the privates; and had our young Ensign possessed any inclination for his cup or his lass, he would inevitably have fallen a victim to one or both before he had been aware that the fatal clutch of the insidious monster was upon him.

Public sentiment had not then pointed out intemperance as base and demoralizing, neither was it considered at all wrong for a gentleman to indulge occasionally in the greatest inebriation. If any attempted to frown down the practice, he was silenced by an invitation to "drink a single drop," and having tasted that single drop, the moralist was too often left "perfectly happy" beneath the table as an example to all who should dare to disturb the rules of good-fellowship.

The expense and privation of the army, and the exclusion from those refining associations daily encountered at the firesides and in the parlors of the civilized, in a measure urged the young officers to frequent, and oftentimes, to alarming extents. The restraint of the fair, the beautiful, the virtuous and the accomplished was not upon them, and they launched into excesses from which they would have shrunk in the quiet of their peaceful homes.

Our young soldier had not entered upon his arduous profession with the mere intention of spending his time in drinking and idling. Far nobler were the sentiments he entertained of what should be the life of a soldier. He soon perceived that he was in a school where advancement depended upon his own bravery, and where he could not expect to gain the praise of his superiors except by regular habits and strict discipline. He saw the danger that beset him at a glance, and he had the good sense and solid resolution not to indulge in the vices of the garrison. In this determination he was supported by the advice of Generals ST. CLAIR and WILKINSON. He resisted all temptations thrown in his way, and thus early laid the foundation of those habits of strict soberness which he has retained through his long and useful life, and by which he has been enabled to encounter all manner of hardships, and yet to enjoy a strong and vigorous constitution.

Soon after his arrival at Fort Washington it became necessary to dispatch a train of pack horses to Fort Hamilton, about thirty miles distant, upon the great Miami. This train was under the charge of a body of soldiers from the fort, and the whole was placed under the command of our boy soldier. This was the first charge confided to his care. Though the distance was short, the state of the country and the thousands of savages peopling the whole forest, rendered the enterprize extremely perilous; and constant exposure required uninterrupted watchfulness, and much more thought, attention and wisdom than can often be found in a lad not yet out of his teens. This service was performed with great credit to himself, and General ST. CLAIR openly acknowledged his pleasure at the success of his young officer, bestowing upon him the warmest praise and commendation. He rapidly gained the entire confidence of his officers, and in 1792, was promoted to the rank of lieutenant.

In May of the year last mentioned, General WAYNE repaired to Pittsburgh, for the purpose of organizing his army. The manner in which he proceeded and the arduous duties he required of his officers and privates, we have already mentioned in a preceding chapter. Such however was the state of the army that he did not consider his men sufficiently disciplined for a march until the 27th of Nov., of the same year.

Having every thing prepared, upon that day he began to move his army, but when only twenty-two miles from Pittsburgh, and about seven miles above the mouth of Beaver river he stopped and encamped for the winter, on the Ohio. Here huts were erected for the whole force, the soldiers going into the comfortable buildings first, and the commander and his officers remaining in tents until all the privates were accommodated in snug quarters. This position was strongly fortified and received the name of Legionville. With the enemy almost surrounding the place, the officers and men were obliged to be on the alert, and the most vigorous watchfulness was constantly observed.

This act of WAYNE has been generally passed over with too slight a notice, but we must here endeavour to do justice to the sagacious warrior. This army, as we have already stated, was formed mostly of new recruits. Many had deserted before they reached the fort. Inexperience and dreadful tales of the blood-thirsty savages they were to encounter, had made many of them timorous. WAYNE disciplined them well before he left Pittsburgh, but he was not yet confident of their bravery before an enemy. He wished to instil into their minds a dependence upon self. If he had remained locked up at Pittsburgh during the winter, it is hardly probable that any thing would have occurred to call forth their energies. He wisely resolved to occupy a more exposed position, where an occasional brush, in which he knew that he must always be successful, would inspire the soldiers with that confidence in themselves which he wished to establish, while it might serve to prove that the Indians were neither immortal nor invincible.

WAYNE had received instructions from WASHINGTON to conciliate the friendly tribes, and so soon as the army was fairly established at Legionville the commander-in-chief despatched an invitation to CORNPLANTER and NEW ARROW, who were the principal chiefs of the SIX NATIONS, to meet him at the garrison. In March, 1793, the chiefs came in, bringing with them BIG TREE and old GUASUTHA. It was on this occasion that CORNPLANTER gave the toast respecting the Ohio river, which we have already quoted. The friendly Indians desired a fixed boundary between the whites and themselves, and such wish appeared neither unnatural nor unreasonable, so far as the tribes themselves were concerned. If these chiefs determined that the Ohio should be the Rubicon, what could be expected from those resolved upon a bloody war?

A large territory north and west of that river had been transferred to Government by treaties and honorable purchase; Congress had guaranteed this property to the officers and soldiers of the revolution, and a large portion of it was already taken up by actual settlement. Yet the Indians were now instructed by their British allies to demand the relinquishment and evacuation of all that beautiful country. The United States could not comply with the terms laid down by the chiefs, though the refusal produced an inevitable and destructive war. The contest was not one for which the Americans could be censured, but was rendered unavoidable by the demands of the savages. It was necessary on other grounds—to teach the Indian wisdom and to restrain his cruel propensities—to destroy forever the dangerous interference of a secret and insidious enemy in Europe, who, having been thoroughly scorched by his own imprudence, was now endeavoring to induce his rude and untutored ally to put his finger into the fire merely that there might be a proper sympathy between the two.

In WAYNE's despatches to government from Legionville, much more confidence was expressed than had previously marked his communications from Pittsburgh. His severe discipline had produced the desired effect, and he felt perfectly safe in his men. The government proposed the appointment of commissioners to treat with the Indians, to which the commander jocosely replied, that he desired to be present at the convention with twenty-five hundred of *his* commissioners, "with not a single Quaker among them." Adding that if such were the case, "I feel confident an honorable peace would be the result."

Haring procured a suitable number of boats for the purpose, he broke up his garrison at Legionville on the 30th of April, 1793, and conveyed his army down the river to Fort Washington, where Lieutenant HARRISON joined the legion.

CHAPTER V.

Peace Commissioners appointed and the army detained at Fort Washington—Removal of the Army to Greenville—Attack on a convoy of provisions—Possession taken of Fort Recovery—Harrison volunteers his services—Receives the public thanks of the Commander-in-chief—A veteran's opinion of Harrison—Suicide of Big-Tree—Harrison inspects the troops—Acts of Great Britain—Occupation of Fort Massac—Preparations for an active campaign.

THE Indians having expressed a desire for peace, the government appointed General LINCOLN, Colonel PICKERING, and BEVERLY RANDOLPH, to meet the chiefs at Sandusky still earnestly desiring to treat the savages with mercy, and determined to give them every opportunity for an amicable adjustment of the prevailing difficulties. In consequence of this movement, General WAYNE was detained at Fort Washington.

Another reason for the delay was the difficulty in procuring reinforcements and supplies, yet active preparations were continually being made for the approaching campaign. The General devoted the whole of his time to perfecting his troops in martial discipline, fully aware that the pending negotiations would not terminate satisfactorily to the government. He made great exertions to procure an ample supply of provisions, and to call in the aid of one thousand mounted volunteers from Kentucky. He left no measure untried which could in any way benefit the garrison, and though he was obliged to attend to much of the detail of the business in person, yet true to his country, he persevered in his exertions until he found his army in a state of comfort and security.

He remained in his quarters until the 7th of October, when he commenced a march, and six days after took up a position on the south west branch of the Miami, six miles beyond Fort Jefferson, and eighty from Fort Washington. To this situation he gave the name of Greenville, and fortified it so as to render it perfectly secure and impregnable to any force which could possibly be brought against him in the wilderness.

On the 17th, an attack was made upon a convoy of provisions, consisting of ninety men, under Lieutenant LOWRY and Ensign BOYD. The greater part of the escort fled on the first discharge, and these two officers, with thirteen others, non-commissioned officers and privates, bravely fell after an obstinate resistance against a superior force.

The Kentucky mounted volunteers reached Greenville shortly after this unfortunate occurrence, but as their services were not likely to be required during the winter, they were directed to return.

December 23d, a detachment of artillery and infantry, under the command of Major Burbeck, was despatched to take possession of the ground upon which ST. CLAIR and his gallant army had been so terribly defeated on the 4th of November, two years before. Lieutenant HARRISON, was not drafted for this expedition, but longing for more active employment, he volunteered for the service, and his assistance was accepted by the commander.

The battle field was soon in the hands of the soldiers, notwithstanding the inclemency of the season, and a fortification was immediately erected, to which the name of Fort Recovery was given. The bones of the murdered soldiers were carefully collected and interred with military honors. The same pieces of artillery lost on the fatal 4th of November, 1791, were recovered, and from their thunder belching mouths, three times three discharges were fired over the remains of the western heroes.

Upon the return of the troops a general order was issued, thanking the officers and men for their "soldierly and exemplary good conduct during their late arduous tour of duty, and the cheerfulness with which they surmounted every difficulty." In the same order we find the following compliment to Lieutenant HARRISON.

"The Commander-in-chief also requests Major MILLS, Captains DE BUTTS and BUTLER, Lieutenant HARRISON, and Dr. SCOTT, to accept his best thanks for their voluntary aid and services on this occasion."

When Mr. HARRISON first entered the service, he was advised by his friends, and even by the new acquaintances he made at Fort Washington, to relinquish the idea of remaining where he would be constantly subject to the most fatiguing duties. The arguments urged to induce him to retire were his extreme youth, his early habits of study, his slight frame and delicate constitution. He had not the appearance of a warrior, or one who could embrace the rude life of a soldier of the wilderness, without injury or ruin to his health. So well convinced were his associates of the impossibility of his undergoing the hardships of the service, that in a body they besought him to resign his commission.

"I would as soon have thought of putting my wife in the service as this boy," writes an old soldier of ST. CLAIR, who was at the fort when MR. HARRISON first made his appearance in the army. "But I have been out with him," continues the veteran, "and I find those smooth cheeks are on a wise head, and that slight frame is almost as tough as my own weather-beaten carcase."

Modest and retiring, when objections were made to his form, he would only reply, "Try me." He was tried. He was often tried, but never found wanting. His constitution hardened with his life, and he was soon able to encounter as much fatigue and privation as any man in the fort, and the reader has already perceived that the boy commanded the attention of men, and his courage, prowess and talents were publicly and gratefully acknowledged by his commander.

Shortly after the occupation of Fort Recovery, a message was received by the Commander-in-chief from the Indians, proposing a negotiation for the adjustment of all controversies; and although WAYNE was satisfied that the overture was only made with the intention of gaining time, yet, aware of the President's desire to avoid the destruction of life, he felt himself obliged to acquiesce in the measure and to open a treaty. He only required of the Indians the return of all American captives, and gave them thirty days to comply with this demand, and to forward their proposals.

The flag was returned with this pacific message, and the distinguished warrior, BIG TREE, of the Senecas, already mentioned, immediately committed suicide. He was friendly to our cause, and had been the intimate friend of General BUTLER, to whose manes he had sworn to sacrifice three victims. He could not endure the idea of a peace which would prevent him from performing his vow, and therefore, put a period to an existence no longer of any value to himself.

This act created much surprise in the garrison, though it was not without its good effect. The soldiers well knew the cause of the melancholy deed, and it roused them to imitate the example of the uncultivated savage in his devoted friendship, though they did not abandon themselves to such useless despair. They resolved to avenge upon the first opportunity, the merciless slaughter of the heroes who fell at St. Clair's defeat two years previous. This glance of the subject suggested itself immediately to the mind of Lieutenant Harrison, and he made frequent reference to the friendship of Big Tree, for the purpose of inspiring the men with similar feelings.

His repeated appeals, and the strong light in which he placed the character of the Indian chief, soon wrought a complete change in the garrison, and made the soldiers eager for a battle, that a bloody sacrifice might be offered to the shades of their murdered brethren.

Great Britain still manifested a hostile spirit against our country. She seized upon every opportunity to chastise her once rebellious colonies. Her fleet broke in upon our commerce and impressed our men. A speech of Lord Dorchester, calculated to influence and encourage the Indians, was freely circulated among the tribes. She refused to evacuate the posts occupied by her army in the north-west, and even erected a fort at the rapids of the Miami.

To increase the troubles, combinations were forming in Kentucky to invade Louisiana, and the governor of the latter had advanced within our territory, and thrown up a fortification at the Chickasaw Bluffs. The Indians again refused to treat, and Wayne found it necessary to open a correspondence with the Governor of Kentucky, and to garrison Fort Massac, on the Ohio, sixty miles above its confluence with the Mississippi.

Active preparations were now recommenced, and the Commander-in-chief waited only the arrival of the mounted volunteers from Kentucky, to begin his march toward the enemy. The soldiers had acquired confidence in themselves, and their general knew he had no longer any thing to apprehend from a decided action. He expected that English soldiers led by their proper officers, would join the Indian forces in case of an engagement, but his own men were so well drilled and disciplined, that this thought produced no fear as to the result.

CHAPTER VI.

Assault upon Fort Recovery—The enemy repulsed—Erection of Fort Defiance—Wayne's overtures to the Indians rejected—Little Turtle's opinion of Gen. Wayne—Wayne's account of the battle of the 20th of August, 1794—His praise of Harrison—The exposure of the aid-de-camp.

AN escort of riflemen and dragoons, under the command of Major M'MAHAN, was attacked under the guns of Fort Recovery, and a general assault made upon that post, June 30th, 1794. A large force of British officers and soldiers were mingled with the Indians in this engagement, aiding and directing the movements of the whole. The onset was repeatedly renewed, and the assailants were as often driven back in disorder and confusion. The foe numbered about fifteen hundred men, and his loss is said to have been very great. The fight was obstinate, but the enemy was eventually completely routed, and victory perched upon the star-splangled banner.

In July, General SCOTT again joined the army, with his daring mounted volunteers from Kentucky, and on the 8th of August, General WAYNE advanced about 70 miles beyond Greenville, and occupied a position at Grand Glaize, in the very midst of the hostile tribes. This movement was executed with the most consummate tact and the greatest rapidity; and had not a soldier deserted and informed the English, the surprise and defeat of the enemy must have immediately followed.

In writing to the Secretary of War, WAYNE expresses himself as having "gained possession of the grand emporium of the hostile Indians in the west, without loss of blood." The country was one of great beauty, and exhibited marks of high and extensive cultivation.

Having erected a fortress at the confluence of the Miami of the Lakes and the Au Glaize, which is called Fort Defiance, and being fully prepared for action at any moment, he resolved to give the Indians still another opportunity to abandon their hostilities. In mentioning this last effort for a conciliation, he expressed his expectation that the tribes would listen to his despatch. "But should war be their choice," said the gallant warrior, "that blood be upon their own heads. America shall no longer be insulted with impunity. To an all powerful and just God, I therefore commit myself and my gallant army."

The proposals were rejected, although LITTLE TURTLE, who had planned and led the attack at the defeat of ST. CLAIR, urged his Indians to embrace the terms. In his appeal to them, he used the following language, in speaking of General WAYNE:

"We have beaten the enemy twice under separate commanders. We cannot expect the same good fortune to attend us always. The Americans are now led by a chief who never sleeps:—the night and the day are alike to him, and during all the time he has been marching upon our villages, notwithstanding the watchfulness of our young men, we have never been able to surprize him. Think well of it. There is something whispers me it would be prudent to listen to his offers of peace."

The day after this speech was delivered, a splendid engagement took place, which resulted in the complete overthrow of the enemy. As this battle was of the greatest importance, we give the official account transmitted to the Secretary of War by the commander-in-chief.

HEAD QUARTERS,
Grand Glaize, 28th August, 1794.

"SIR:—It is with infinite pleasure that I now announce to you the brilliant success of the federal army under my command, in a general action with the combined force of the hostile Indians, and a considerable number of the volunteers and militia of Detroit, on the 20th instant, on the banks of the Miami in the vicinity of the British post and garrison, at the foot of the rapids.

"The army advanced from this place on the 15th instant, and arrived at Roche de Bout on the 18th; the 19th we were employed in making a temporary post for the reception of our stores and baggage, and in reconnoitering the position of the enemy, who were encamped behind a thick bushy wood, and the British fort.

"At 8 o'clock on the 20th, the army again advanced in columns, agreeably to the standing order of march; the legion on the right flank, covered by the Miami,—one brigade of mounted volunteers on the left, under Brigadier General TODD, and the other in the rear, under Brigadier General BARBEE:— a select battalion of mounted volunteers moved in front of the legion, commanded by Major PRICE, who was directed to keep sufficiently advanced—so as to give timely notice for the troops to form, in case of action—it being yet undetermined whether the Indians would decide for peace or war. After advancing about five miles, Major Price's corps received so severe a fire from the enemy, who were secreted in the woods and high grass, as to compel them to retreat.

"The legion was immediately formed in two lines, principally in a close, thick wood, which extended for miles on our left; and for a very considerable distance in front, the ground being covered with old fallen timber, probably occasioned by a tornado, which rendered it impracticable for cavalry to act with effect, and afforded the enemy the most favorable covert for their savage mode of warfare, they were formed in three lines within supporting distance of each other, and extending nearly two miles, at right angles with the river.

"I soon discovered from the weight of the fire, and the extent of their lines, that the enemy were in full force in front, in possession of their favorite ground, and endeavoring to turn our left flank. I therefore gave orders for the second line to advance, to support the first, and directed Major General SCOTT to gain and turn the right flank of the savages, with the whole of the mounted volunteers, by a circuitous route; at the same time I ordered the front line to advance with trailed arms and rouse the Indians from their coverts at the point of the bayonet; and when up, to deliver a close and well directed fire on their backs, followed by a brisk charge, so as not to give them time to load again. I also ordered Captain Miss. CAMPBELL, who commanded the legionary cavalry, to turn the left flank of the enemy next the river, which afforded a favorable field for that corps to act in. All these orders were obeyed with spirit and promptitude; but such was the impetuosity of the charge of the first line of infantry, that the Indians and Canadian militia and volunteers were driven from all their coverts in so short a time, that although every exertion was used by the officers of the second line of the legion, and by Generals SCOTT, TODD and BARBEE, of the mounted volunteers, to gain their proper positions; yet but a part of each could get up in season to participate in the action; the enemy being driven, in the course of one hour, more than two miles, through the thick woods already mentioned, by less than one half their numbers.

"From every account, the enemy amounted to two thousand combatants; the troops actually engaged against them were short of nine hundred. This horde of savages, with their allies abandoned themselves to flight, and dispersed with terror and dismay, leaving our victorious army in full and quiet possession of the field of battle, which terminated under the influence of the guns of the British garrison, as you will observe by the inclosed correspondence between Major CAMPBELL, the commandant, and myself, upon the occasion.

"The bravery and conduct of every officer belonging to the army, from the generals down to the ensigns, merit my highest approbation. There were, however, some whose rank and situation placed their conduct in a very conspicuous point of view, and which I observed with pleasure and the most lively gratitude: among whom I beg leave to mention Brigadier General WILKINSON, and Colonel HAMTRANCK, the commandants of the right and left wings of the legion, whose brave example inspired the troops; and to these I must add the names of my faithful and gallant aids-de-camp, Captains DE BUTTS and T. LEWIS, and Lieutenant HARRISON, who, with the adjutant general, Major MILLS, rendered the most essential services by communicating my orders in every direction, and by their conduct and bravery exciting the troops to press for victory. Lieutenant COVINGTON, upon whom the command of the cavalry now devolved, cut down two savages with his own hand, and Lieutenant WEBB one, in turning the enemy's left flank.

"The wounds received by Captains SLOUGH and PRIOR, and Lieutenants CAMPBELL, SMITH (an extra aid-de-camp to General WILKINSON) of the legionary infantry, and Captain VAN RENSELLAER, of the dragoons, and Captain RAWLINS, Lieutenant M'KENNEY, and Ensign DUNCAN, of the mounted volunteers, bear an honorable testimony to their bravery and conduct.

"Captains H. LEWIS and BROCK, with their companies of light infantry, had to sustain an unequal fire for some time, which they supported with fortitude. In fact, every officer and soldier who had an opportunity to come into action, displayed that true bravery which will always insure success.

"And here permit me to declare, that I never discovered more true spirit and anxiety for action, than appeared to pervade the whole of the mounted volunteers; and I am well persuaded that had the enemy maintained their favorite ground but for one half hour longer, they would have most severely felt the prowess of that corps.

"But whilst I pay this just tribute to the living I must not forget the gallant dead; among whom we have to lament the early death of those worthy and brave officers, Captain Miss. CAMPBELL of the dragoons, and Lieutenant TOWLES of the light infantry of the legion, who fell in the first charge.

"Inclosed is a particular return of the killed and wounded—the loss of the enemy was more than double that of the federal army. The woods were strewed for a considerable distance with the dead bodies of the Indians, and their white auxiliaries; the latter armed with British muskets and bayonets.

"We remained three days and nights on the banks of the Miami, in front of the field of battle, during which all the houses and cornfields were consumed and destroyed for a considerable distance, both above and below Fort Miami, as well as within pistol-shot of that garrison, who were compelled to remain tacit spectators of this general devastation and conflagration—among which were the houses, stores and property of Colonel M'KEE, the British Indian Agent, and principal stimulator of the war now existing between the United States and the savages.

"The army returned to this place on the 27th by easy marches, laying waste the villages and cornfields for about fifty miles on each side of the Miami; there remain yet a number of villages, and a great quantity of corn to be consumed or destroyed, upon Au Glaize and the Miami, which will be effected in the course of a few days. In the interim we shall improve Fort Defiance, and as soon as the escort returns with the necessary supplies from Greenville and Fort Recovery, the army will proceed to the Miami villages, in order to accomplish the object of the campaign.

"It is, however, not improbable that the enemy may make one more desperate effort against the army; as it is said that a reinforcement was hourly expected at Fort Miami, from Niagara, as well as numerous tribes of Indians, living on the margins and lakes. This is a business rather to be wished for than dreaded, as long as the army remains in force. Their numbers will only tend to confuse the savages, and the victory will be more complete and decisive—and which may eventually insure a permanent and happy peace.

"Under these impressions, I have the honor to be,
"Your most obedient,
"And very humble servant,
"ANTHONY WAYNE.

"The Hon. Major-General KNOX,
Secretary of War."

It will be seen by this communication of the Commander-in-chief, that the service in which Mr. HARRISON had engaged was no child's play. Men were expected to do their duty, and they were thrown forward by their heroic general where they were compelled to rely upon their own prowess and bravery. The open fire and rapid charge were new and dangerous movements, originating with MAD ANTHONY, and he fully proved in this campaign that *his* was the true system of battling with the Indians. While the savage was permitted to stand quietly behind his tree, and load and fire in safety, every ball carried death; but when an impetuous assault drove him from his shelter, and destroyed the power of using the rifle on which he depended altogether, or nearly so, he lost all hope and abandoned himself to a flight, oftentimes as dangerous as precipitate.

In the engagement recorded, Lieutenant HARRISON acted as aid, in which employment he was constantly exposed, being despatched with orders to almost every quarter of the field, and frequently compelled to ride into the thickest of the battle, and before the incessant discharge of the enemy, to make his communications to the officers.

The Campaign of WAYNE was an admirable school for a young and daring soldier, and through his whole life, our brave lieutenant gave continual evidence that he had profited by the lessons he there received.

CHAPTER VII.

Conduct of Major Campbell—Survey of Fort Miami—Observation and conduct of Buckongahelas—He and the Turtle renounce the English—Negotiations opened—Treaty concluded—Effect produced in England by Wayne's Victory—Emigration renewed—Mr. Harrison promoted to a Captaincy, and placed in command of Fort Washington—French intrigues—Powers conferred upon Captain Harrison—His marriage.

IMMEDIATELY after the action recorded in the preceding chapter, the Commander-in-chief received a communication from Major CAMPBELL, the British commandant of the Fort Miami, requesting to be informed, whether he was to consider the American army as enemies, being ignorant of any war existing between the King, his master, and the United States. The correspondence which ensued, and which the reader will find in the appendix to this volume, determined General WAYNE to examine Fort Miami thoroughly, and if necessary, take it. He had authority for such a course in case the fort at all obstructed his operations, and his army was just in the right spirit for the enterprize. Flushed with the recent glorious victory, his men would have marched directly to the mouths of the British cannon, had he but given the word. He had the sagacity to perceive that such an enterprize might again involve the States with Great Britain, and therefore concluded to take no notice of it unless he found the measure absolutely necessary for the success of his campaign.

The work was thoroughly examined. The general himself, accompanied by a troop of dragoons, approached within one hundred yards of the fort, where he halted a few moments to survey the spot. Accompanied by his aids, DE BUTTS and HARRISON, he presently moved slowly on toward the fortress. When within sixty yards of one of the bastions, the English gunners were seen leaning over the cannon, with lighted torches in their hands. One piece was brought to a recover, ready to fire. HARRISON drew the attention of the general to the circumstance, remarking that he would be shot immediately. The general cooly replied, that the sentinel dare not fire.

The next moment WILKINSON came up with his staff, at a hand gallop, and an officer was seen in the bastion, endeavoring to prevent the soldiers from firing. WAYNE checked his horse, and slowly retired, followed by his friends. Letter, No. III., in the appendix refers to this.

The spirit of the Indians was much subdued by the battle, and they began to examine into the conduct of the British with the closest scrutiny.

DAWSON states that there were two companies of British militia from Detroit, in the engagement, and yet the gates of Fort Miami were shut against the retreating Indians. The great war chief BUCKONGAHELAS was the first to observe this, and he immediately determined to abandon the English. He placed his tribes in canoes and proceeded up the river. Being requested so to do, he landed when near the British fort, and demanded of the officer, "what have you to say to me?" being told that the commanding officer wished to speak with him, he replied, "then he may come here." "He will not do that, and you will not be permitted to pass unless you attend him," was the reply. "What shall prevent me?" demanded the daring savage. "These guns," was the reply, pointing to the English cannon. The answer of the chief was as severe as true, "I fear not your cannon," said he, "after suffering the Americans to defile your spring without daring to fire on them, you cannot expect to frighten BUCKONGAHELAS," and speaking to his men in his own language, he ordered the canoes to be pushed off, and passed the fort unmolested. From that hour he refused to have any communication with the British, and on his death bed in 1804, advised his tribe to rely upon the friendship of the United States.

The TURTLE also renounced the English and became the advocate of peace with the United States; not from fear for he was a stranger to the feeling, but in consequence of the conduct of the British toward their defeated allies. As we shall have occasion hereafter to speak more at large upon the character of this warrior, we leave his defence for the present.

January 1st, 1795, the Indians opened a negotiation for peace, agreeing to surrender all captives—to ratify all former treaties, and to comply with such general terms as should be imposed by General WAYNE. They also gave hostages tor the faithful performance of their obligations.

Shortly after, a treaty was finally concluded at Greenville, by which the Indians relinquished an immense territory to defray the expenses of the war and abandoned certain parts important to the United States. The news of WAYNE's victory reaching England in Nov., 1794, enabled MR. JAY to conclude most advantageously for our government, the negociation which had been long pending between him and Lord GRENVILLE. One important stipulation in JAY's treaty, was the surrender to the United States of all the forts held and occupied by the British, in the north-west, within the jurisdiction of our government. The settlers had now uninterrupted possession of the disputed territory, and emigration rapidly progressed.

Upon the close of the campaign, MR. HARRISON was promoted to a captaincy, though still retaining his rank as aid-de-camp to General WAYNE, and placed in command of Fort Washington, under circumstances which proved the confidence of the commander-in-chief, and the exalted opinion entertained by that officer for the integrity, intrepidity and discretion of his young pupil. The American troops, arms, ammunition and provisions, intended for the forts evacuated by the British, were to be sent to Captain HARRISON, and by him forwarded to their respective stations.

The French intrigues in Kentucky were still going forward for an invasion of Louisiana, and many wealthy and intelligent persons had already connected themselves with the proposed expedition. The object represented to the Americans, and which they earnestly desired was the uninterrupted right to navigate the Mississippi, which the Spanish government at that time denied. General WAYNE still kept up the correspondence with the governor of Kentucky, to which allusion has already been made, and Captain HARRISON was instructed to keep the general advised of all movements toward the south, and to prevent the passage of the boats of the French agents over the river, laden with military stores. Discretionary powers of almost unlimited extent were also given to the young officer, to be used as circumstances might require. "It is no slight evidence," says HALL in his memoir of HARRISON, "of the prudence, ability and intelligence of HARRISON, that at an early age, and with the rank only of Captain, he was selected by the discriminating WAYNE to discharge duties so important, and to exercise a responsibility so delicate. It is enough to say, that in this, as well as on various subsequent trusts reposed in him throughout a long career, he honorably vindicated, by his fidelity and zeal, the choice of the appointing power."

At this time he was just turned of twenty-two years of age, and the talent, fortitude and wisdom of his youth increased with his years and marked every act of his eventful and glorious career. He remained at Fort Washington discharging his arduous and complicated duties with boldness, punctuality and uncommon intelligence; and while there married the daughter of JOHN CLEVES SYMMES, the founder of the Miami settlements. "She has been," says HALL, "the faithful companion of this distinguished patriot, during the various perils and vicissitudes of his eventful life, and still lives to witness the maturity of his fame, and the honors paid him by a grateful country."

CHAPTER VIII.

Captain Harrison leaves the army, and is appointed Secretary of the North-western Territory—Condition of the country—Manner of selling public lands—Mr. Harrison chosen delegate to Congress—He is appointed chairman of a committee to investigate the land laws—Reports a bill—The bill passed—The Territory divided, and Mr. Harrison appointed Governor of the new Territory of Indiana.

ON the death of General WAYNE, which occurred in 1797, Captain HARRISON left the army, and received his first civil appointment, as Secretary of the North-western Territory, and *ex-officio,* Lieutenant Governor. We have gone with him through his early military career, and have seen him even at the age of eighteen, manfully battling with the enemies of his country, and exposing his life constantly and for years after in defence of the border settlements. We have now to view him in a new light—he has in a measure doffed the sword and plume, and brought his mighty intellect to the civil service of his fellow-citizens.

The early settlers of the western wilderness had trials, hardships and privations to endure almost incredible to us of the present day, and the beautiful garden spots now blooming in all the luxury of cultivation, give no idea of the thorn and the oak, the bed of earth and the covering of clouds which were at that time the hourly companions of the hardy pioneers. The forest was their home, and the panther and the wolf, howled the night through, around their rude log tenements. Their food was the game of the woods, which they procured by their rifles, and the only luxury they enjoyed may be said to have been the sleep of the weary. Beside these they still had to encounter the savages, and frequent murders were committed, of the most outrageous character and in cool blood.

All shared alike the privations and labor, and all lived alike in the rough log cabins. With MAD ANTHONY, one of the bravest and most daring soldiers, Mr. HARRISON had learned the art of war. Among the hardiest set of men—

men ready to buffet wind, weather and the beasts of the forest—in a wild, uncultivated district, open to constant and sudden dangers, he commenced the study of civil improvement. He may truly be said, to have begun with the great west, and to have grown with it. He gathered instruction from his association with the farmers, soldiers and pioneers—listened to their wants, and did all in his power to serve and benefit them.

At that time the public lands were disposed of by the government, in tracts of four thousand acres, and an individual could not purchase less. The effect of this erroneous system was, in a measure to exclude actual settlers, while men of fortune could take up large tracts and enter upon splendid speculations by retailing their property in small farms. The men who generally settle a new country ore extremely poor. They go forward with the rifle and axe, and clear their lands and provide food for their families. They are unable to buy large estates, or were they possessed of sufficient means of doing so, they do not want more than they can readily till.

The governmental arrangement we have alluded to, greatly retarded the growth of the western country, and to protect settlers from the enormous exactions of the rich speculator, it became necessary to have new laws for the sale of lands, by which small farms could be purchased immediately from government at the stated prices.

The year following, the North-eastern Territory entered upon the second grade of territorial government, and was entitled to representation by a delegate in Congress. MR. HARRISON had been the first to point out to the people the embarrassment produced by the land law, and they now chose him as their first delegate.

His associates in Congress were men of the first order of intellect, and he here again profited by words of instruction from the lips of the wise. BAYARD, GALLATIN and MARSHALL were men from whom the erudite could still gather knowledge, and the youthful delegate and intrepid soldier, ever ready to learn, listened with eagerness to their profound suggestions.

He soon offered a resolution for the appointment of a committee to investigate and report upon the existing manner of disposing of public lands. Of this committee, he was selected chairman, and "it is believed," says HALL, "this is the only instance in which that distinction has been conferred upon a territorial delegate." He shortly after, reported upon his resolution and also presented a bill, the main clause of which reduced the size of tracts from four thousand acres to alternate half and quarter sections; or, alternate tracts of three hundred and twenty and one hundred and sixty acres. This was for the express purpose of placing purchases within the immediate reach of the farmer and the actual settler.

The report accompanying the bill gave a clear and distinct view of the true position of the population of his territory, and the great disadvantages under which the people labored. It gained for the new delegate a reputation unprecedented for so young a man, and upon his first appearance in the political arena.

When the bill came up for discussion, it was violently attacked by MR. LEE of Virginia, and MR. COOPER, of New York; but the mover alone defended his project, and disclosed a perfect knowledge of his subject. He examined the old system—pointed out its injurious effects—showed that the rich man was benefited by it, and that the poor must and did suffer. He stood before his country, upon the floor of the House of Representatives, the champion of the people—to defend them against the unwarrantable speculations of the wealthy, and to secure to them equal advantages with their rich neighbors. His eloquent argument had the desired effect, and the bill passed the House triumphantly.

The Senate however, refused to pass the bill, and committees of conference were appointed—MR. GALLATIN and MR. HARRISON on the part of the House, and MR. ROSS and MR. BROWN on the part of the Senate. So great was the opposition now, that MR. HARRISON was compelled to submit to a compromise, by which the public lands were thereafter to be sold in alternate whole and half sections, or tracts of six hundred and forty and six hundred and twenty acres.

In producing the report, MR. GALLATIN greatly assisted the western delegate, and as soon as the object was accomplished, MR. HARRISON gave his friend due credit for his valuable assistance. He wished to do so at once, but was prevented by the earnest request of MR. GALLATIN himself.

The bill became an act, and the people of the west have been, we may say, *made* by it. It is stated on good authority, that had the passage of the bill been delayed one year, a large portion of Ohio would have been sold off in four thousand acre tracts to capitalists, to the exclusion of the hardy settlers who have since placed that whole state in her present bright and happy condition.

Mr. Harrison next offered a resolution changing the manner of treating military land-warrants. A committee was appointed, and a proper bill introduced which became a law.

Thus early in life we find Mr. Harrison contending manfully for the rights of the people and practising upon the noble principles laid down by his distinguished father: nor has the son ever for a single moment, lost sight of or neglected to follow the patriotic precepts and example of his honored parent. The success of the delegate was manifest throughout the whole north-western country, and may now be witnessed in the prosperity of millions of intelligent freemen. The part he took gained him great popularity, and the settlers at once forwarded an immense number of petitions, requesting the President to appoint Mr. Harrison governor of the North-western Territory. He himself opposed the object of these petitions, being unwilling to permit his name to come in competition with that of his esteemed and venerable friend, St. Clair.

About this time however, that which now is the State of Ohio, was created a territory by itself, and the remainder of the North-western Territory received the name of Indiana, being erected into a separate government. Having served but one year in Congress, Mr. Harrison was, at the almost universal request of the inhabitants, appointed by the President, governor of the Territory of Indiana.

Mr. Harrison early identified himself with the republican party;—has been, at all times, the champion of the people, and a zealous advocate for the diffusion of the pure principles of democracy. His constant and indefatigable exertions for the people of the west, procured for him that title which has been conferred by general consent—the Father of the North-Western Territory.

CHAPTER IX.

Situation of the Country—Stations—Massacre of a settler's family—British interference—The Governor's powers and duties—The Territory enters upon the second grade of government—The Governor recovers damages against a slanderer—His conduct upon the sale of the libeller's property—He declined fees for Indiana licenses—His pay as Indiana Commissioner—His popularity—Manner of doing public business.

AT the time MR. HARRISON received the appointment of Governor of the Territory of Indiana, that country was under the first form of territorial government, and almost unlimited power was vested in the executive. It was a vast domain including the whole territory of the United States beyond the Mississippi and Ohio, except that which is now the State of Ohio; and from 1803 to 1805, the whole of upper Louisiana was also embraced under the jurisdiction of Governor HARRISON.

The people had no voice whatever in their own affairs. New institutions were to be formed, and all power was delegated to the territorial governor. The population was small, and widely scattered. There were but three settlements of any size in the whole territory—one at the falls of the Ohio, opposite Louisville, another at Vincennes, five hundred miles distant, and the third, the French towns on the Mississippi, extending from Kaskaskia to Cahokia, and two hundred miles from Vincennes.

The intermediate country was the scene of constant difficulties between the Indians and the hunters. Robberies and barbarous murders were almost daily occurrences, and very little security was enjoyed until the close of the war of 1812. In different quarters attacks were frequently made simultaneously, and the most revolting barbarities practised. The only roads between the settlements were paths beaten by the Indians, and the only resting places were log houses, surrounded by palisades, and called stations. We have one account of a man who was travelling west with his wife, two sons and a daughter. Having been detained by an accident, he was unable to reach the station, and posting one of his sons as a guard, he encamped for the night. About midnight, the crack of a rifle roused the father, and seizing his gun, he was about to rush to the aid of his child, when a glimmering tomahawk flashed through the dim light, and buried itself in his body. The Indians had shot the sentry, and now butchered the whole family except the daughter, who was a beautiful girl about sixteen years of age. She was retained, and forced to become the wife of one of the Indian murderers. Two years after she effected her escape, and told the story of the massacre. This is but one case out of hundreds.

The seat of government was at Vincennes, on the Wabash; a town inhabited principally by French people. The British traders carried on an extensive and profitable business with the Indians, and jealous of the increasing population of the new country, pains were taken to prejudice the minds of the savages against our government. The traders were stimulated to this proceeding by their home government, for England could not even yet reconcile the idea of the United States remaining a free country, and preparatory to another war, was anxious to enlist the savage tribes in her favor.

The Governor had all these evils to contend against, and on him chiefly devolved the adoption of such laws of the original states as were deemed necessary. He also appointed all magistrates and other civil officers, and all militia officers below the grade of general. It remained with him also to divide the country into counties and townships. He could pardon. He was the agent and representative of the general government, and could confirm grants of land to a numerous class of individuals, having certain claims specified in the law. The application was made directly to the Governor, and his signature was alone sufficient to confirm a title unquestionable before any legal tribunal. Although this power was so susceptible of abuse; such was the prudence of Governor HARRISON, and such his scrupulous attention to the interests of the public, and delicate regard for his honor, that his duty was discharged without a single suspicion of his integrity.

MR. JEFFERSON appointed Governor HARRISON, sole commissioner for treating with the Indians. Here his time was wholly occupied and he had the disbursement of large sums of money, appropriated by Congress for annuities to the tribes and for purchasing lands. He conducted this trust with great discreetness, and acquired an uncommon influence over the Indians. His administration is declared to have been nearly a succession of treaties,[2] by one of which he secured to the United States fifty one millions of acres of the richest country in the west, and the most valuable mineral region in the Union.

The Territory entered upon the second grade of government in 1805, and by this the people were allowed a legislature. They elected members to the lower house, and this branch nominated ten persons, out of whom Congress chose five, who constituted the less numerous branch.

Although this change deprived the governor of much power and patronage, yet he earnestly advocated the alteration, and felt greatly relieved when the new legislature assumed many of the enormous responsibilities, which previously had rested alone upon the executive.

Governor HARRISON brought a suit against a person who had thrown out some malicious hints in reference to his negotiations with the Indians. The charge was fresh—the testimony at hand, and a complete investigation was had before the Supreme Court. Two judges left the bench—one, a friend of the Governor, and the other of the defendant.

The trial had not far advanced, when the defendant's council gave up the plea of justifications and contended only for mitigation of damages. The jury in one hour, returned a verdict of four thousand dollars damages for the Governor. This was an enormous verdict for a new country. The defendant's property was sold, and bought in by the Governor's agent. Shortly after two thirds of the property were returned by the Governor to his slanderer, and the remainder was given to the orphans of some of the soldiers who had fallen in battle.

So far from ever attempting to benefit himself, although he might have done so with perfect justness and integrity in many instances, he refused every opportunity to profit by his own powers. Nay, further: he even went so far as to sometimes refuse that which was his honest due under the laws, lest some one might accuse him wrongfully, or that the mere appearance might have an injurious effect upon others. When appointed ex-officio Governor of upper Louisiana, he knew that the president earnestly wished to convince the inhabitants of the newly acquired territory of the corruption under which

---

[2] Hall.

they had lived and the fairness and honor of our government; and to aid the intentions of Mr. Jefferson, Governor Harrison declined receiving the fees for Indian licenses, which would have brought him at least two or three thousand dollars, and to which he was justly entitled by law.

While acting as commissioner his compensation was six dollars a day and expenses, and it was left with himself to say when he was acting under his commission, and when under that of superintendent; and although he held the first commission for eleven years, and during that time negotiated no less than thirteen treaties, yet the whole charge made for such services in that time amounted only to about five thousand dollars.

He also repeatedly refused to purchase property or to become interested in the purchases of others, though frequently solicited, and having constant opportunity to amass splendid fortunes.[3]

The various addresses of Governor Harrison to the legislature, show a remarkable clearness of perception and perspicuity of style. He never neglected the recommendation of any measure which he considered necessary to be adopted; and never advised the passage of any act, without, giving the most profound and convincing reasons for his advocacy. To enable the public to judge of his abilities, several specimens of his writings are introduced in the appendix.

The extensive and almost unlimited powers given to territorial governors, render it difficult for them to maintain anything like popularity. The people are apt to become dissatisfied with being ruled by a governor in whose appointment they have no choice. They become suspicious of his intentions and impatient under his authority. These feelings are particularly visible among the settlers of a new country. Men who make themselves—who hew their way through life, and by a natural independence and stubborn integrity are constantly accustomed to examine for themselves—are not often content to remain under an authority not of their own selection. This repugnance however, was never felt toward Governor Harrison. His manner was conciliating, and he always commanded respect, while he also engaged the warm affections of the people. He used the extensive authority placed in his hands, with wisdom and discretion. In appointments to office under him, he

---

[3] See a letter from General Harrison, dated "North Bend, Oct. 18, 1839." in the appendix.

always consulted the people and selected those who enjoyed the confidence of their fellow-citizens. To this principle he sacrificed even personal and political feeling—frequently appointing to office men in every way opposed to himself.

During nearly the whole of his life he has been intrusted with immense sums of money, yet he so managed his accounts as never to have a large amount on hand, while he skillfully contrived to save the government the risk and expense of transporting money to the west, by transmitting to Washington drafts and receipts at the same time.

CHAPTER X.

Extract from the Governor's first message to the Indiana Legislature—The Governor's exertions in behalf of the Indians—Conduct of Buckongahelas—Notice of Little Turtle—His endeavours to prevent the sale of liquor to his tribe—He is inoculated, and takes some matter to inoculate other Indians.

GOVERNOR HARRISON constantly endeavored to reconcile the Indians to their condition, and to supply as far as possible, their necessities. Measures were adopted by which their communications with the British were greatly abridged, and they were forced to procure from the Americans their arms and ammunition. Large sums of money were appropriated to their use by the United States, and agents were employed to instruct them in such acts of civilized life as they were capable of receiving.

A law had been passed by Congress, to prevent the sale of spirituous liquors to the savages, but it had not the desired effect, being so open that constant evasions were made upon its tenor. In Governor HARRISON's first message to the new legislature of the territory, in speaking upon this subject, he used the following eloquent and feeling language:

"The humane and benevolent intentions of the government, however, will forever be defeated, unless effectual measures be devised to prevent the sale of ardent spirits to those unhappy people. The law which has been passed by Congress for that purpose, has been found ineffectual, because its operation has been construed to relate to the Indian country exclusively. In calling your attention to this subject, gentlemen, I am persuaded that it is unnecessary to remind you, that the article of compact makes it your duty to attend to it. The interests of your constituents, the interests of the miserable Indians, and your own feelings, will sufficiently urge you to take it into your most serious consideration, and provide the remedy which is to save thousands of your fellow-creatures. You are witnesses to the abuses; you have seen our towns crowded with furious and drunken savages, our streets flowing with their blood, their arms, and clothing bartered for the liquor that destroys them, and their miserable women and children enduring all the extremities of cold and hunger. So destructive has the progress of intemperance been among them, that whole villages have been swept away. A miserable remnant is all that remains to mark the names and situations of many numerous and warlike tribes. In the energetic language of one of their orators, it is a dreadful conflagration, which spreads misery and devastation throughout their country, and threatens the annihilation of the whole race. Is it then to be admitted as a political axiom, that the neighborhood of a civilized nation is incompatible with the existence of savages? Are the blessings of our republican government only to be felt by ourselves? And are the natives of North America to experience the same fate with their brethren of the southern continent? It is with you, gentlemen, to divert from those children of nature the ruin that hangs over them. Nor can I believe that the time will be considered mispent, which is devoted to an object so consistent with the spirit of Christianity and with the principles of republicanism."

The Governor now exerted every power within his reach to induce the Indians to remain quiet, and in friendship with the United States. His philanthropic intentions were much assisted by the territorial legislature and by many personal friends, and he had the satisfaction for some time, of seeing the happiest results flow from his benevolent designs. He sent out repeatedly for the chiefs of various tribes, and succeeded in concluding with many, treaties advantageous to the United States. This indeed, he had done while the territory was under his own immediate control, and he continued his efforts to relieve and pacify the savages during the whole time he held his office.

In 1803, a council of chiefs was held at Fort Wayne, for the purpose of ratifying a negotiation for land, which had been proposed at a former meeting at Vincennes. BUCKONGAHELAS, the DELAWARE chief, of whom we have before spoken, was present at this council, and caused some trouble to the Governor. The POTAWATAMIES and some of the MIAMIES boldly seconded the Executive in all his propositions, but the DELAWARES and SHAWANEES opposed every movement, and when the Vincennes transaction was alluded to, the latter were filled with wrath and indignation. "The respected BUCKONGAHELAS," says DAWSON, "so far forgot himself that he interrupted the Governor, and declared with vehemence, that nothing that was done at Vincennes was binding upon the Indians; and that he had then with him a chief who had been present at the transfer made by the PIANKISHAWS to the DELAWARES of all the country between the Ohio and White rivers, more than thirty years before.

"The SHAWANEES went still further, and behaved with so much insolence, that the Governor was obliged to tell them that they were undutiful and rebellious children, and that he would withdraw his protection from them until they had learned to behave themselves with more propriety. These chiefs immediately left the council house in a body."

The SHAWANEES afterward submitted—the Governor put down all opposition and carried his point. BUCKONGAHELAS was as obstinate as ever, though at his death, which occurred the following year, he advised his tribe to desert the English and rely upon the friendship of the United States. He was a daring fellow, and had no mean opinion of himself. At the council of Fort McIntoch, when the American officers and Indian chiefs had assembled, it was he, who, without deigning to notice any others, advanced to the General, and taking him by the hand, said, "I thank the Great Spirit for having this day brought together two such great warriors as BUCKONGAHELAS and General CLARK."

Many other hostile chiefs were through the wisdom and care of Governor HARRISON, brought to consider the United States the government to which they should cling, and they abandoned forever all communication with the British.

It was the LITTLE TURTLE who principally assisted at the council in 1803, and he appears to have renounced all connection with the English soon after the treaty of Greenville. He frequently visited Philadelphia and Washington after this, and having settled upon Eel River, about twenty miles from Fort Wayne, a comfortable house was erected for him, and he was furnished with every reasonable accommodation by the American government. The vice of intemperance raged with great fury among his people, and he was exceedingly gratified with the course pursued by Governor HARRISON to prevent the sale of spiritous liquors to the Indians. He had seen hundreds of his best and bravest warriors at one time, in war, surprised and massacred in their cups, on the very ground where he had obtained his most signal victories. His pride could not brook the idea that his people should become beasts, and he took every measure in his power to stay the destruction pouring over them. He argued and remonstrated, but his influence with his tribes was much weakened.

About the time of the council at Fort Wayne, he went before the legislature of Kentucky, and made an appeal to them in person, through his friend and interpreter, Captain WELLS. He also made a powerful address to the legislature of Ohio. He begged both to interfere to prevent the traders from selling liquor to his people. The traders he described forcibly: "They stripped the poor Indians," said he, "of skins, gun, blanket, everything,—while his squaw and the children dependant on him lay starving and shivering in his wigwam."

He did all he could for his people, but his exertions were in a great degree useless. In 1801, or 1802, while in Washington, at the solicitation of the President, he and several of his warriors were inoculated. When he went home, he took a quantity of vaccine matter, and administered the potent remedy for the small-pox, in person. Soon after a deputation from his tribe visited Washington to procure more of the matter.

Several other chiefs represented to Governor HARRISON the ruin which was desolating their towns through the influence of spiritous liquors. Early in this volume we represented the excesses of the American army at Fort Washington, when Mr. HARRISON first joined the troops, and his own resolution to withstand all temptations to drink. He had a dreadful picture before, both among his countrymen and the tribes around the fort. He saw all the evils of this pernicious vice, and from that moment endeavored, not only to prohibit the sale of liquor to the Indians, but by advice and remonstrance to prevail upon the savages to abandon a custom, which carried with it nothing but disease, disgrace and death.

For the purpose of showing his opinion on this subject in his own words, we copied the extract from his address to the legislature, in the beginning of this chapter. The same inveterate opposition to liquor has marked the course of his life.

CHAPTER XI.

Governor Harrison's treatment of the Indians—His writings and speeches—Complimentary notices—Conduct of the hunters—Conduct of the British agents—The Governor's influence over the Indians—Attempt upon his life.

In our appendix will be found several specimens of Mr. Harrison's writings, and we refer to them with a conscious pride in the talent they display. They are variously selected, that the reader may make himself perfectly acquainted with the sentiments of this distinguished man in the many and important situations he occupied. The whole tenor of his official communications exhibit the cultivated intellect, the reflecting mind, and the feeling heart. His constant anxiety to forward the interests of all who came under his jurisdiction, and his unremitted exertions to ameliorate the condition of the savage tribes, will forever redound to his honor and hand down his name to posterity with love and veneration.

He never refused to hear the complaints of the Indians, but met their chiefs with that dignity and kindness which became his station. He listened patiently to the story of their wrongs, and replied to them in language conciliating and endearing. He promised to do all in his power to gratify their reasonable demands, and he never broke his promise. Though many of the tribes behaved with treachery to him, yet he was always calm, moderate and forbearing. Bold, energetic and fearless in the field, he was nevertheless, as a civil magistrate humane and considerate.

In speaking of his character, Mr. Hall uses the following complimentary language. "He did not neglect any of the various civil duties which were confided to his care. All the departments of the government were modelled under his direction; and in his communications to the legislature, the various subjects of legislation were freely discussed. His speeches were frank and manly; and he writes with the ease, correctness and precision, of one who was accustomed to think with clearness, and who possessed in a high degree the faculty of fluent expression. Few of our public documents will be found to be couched in better language than those of Governor HARRISON.

When first appointed Governor of the Territory of Indiana, MR. HARRISON openly declared his determination not to hold the station a moment longer than his administration should be satisfactory to the people; and at their request he received his successive re-appointments from Presidents, ADAMS, JEFFERSON and MADISON. The following were the sentiments of the citizens of St. Louis, when their connection with Indiana was about to terminate:—

"To his Excellency WILLIAM HENRY HARRISON, Governor, and the honorable the Judges of the Indiana Territory.

"GENTLEMEN:

"An arduous public service assigned you by the general government of the United States, is about to cease. The eve of the anniversary of American Independence will close the scene; and on that celebrated festival will be organized, under most auspicious circumstances, a government for the Territory of Louisiana. Local situation and circumstances forbid the possibility of a permanent political connection. This change, however congenial to our wishes, will not take effect without a respectful expression of sentiment to you, gentlemen, for your assiduity, attention, and disinterested punctuality, in the temporary administration of your government of Louisiana.

"St. Louis, July 2, 1805."

Governor HARRISON was presented with an address from the officers of the militia in the district of St. Louis, at the same time. The address concludes thus:

"Accept, Sir, these sentiments as the pledge of our affectionate attachment to you, and to the magnanimous policy by which you have been guided. May the chief magistrate of the American nation duly estimate your worth and talents, and long keep you in a station where you have it in your power to gain hearts by virtuous actions, and promulgate laws among men who know how to respect you, and are acquainted with their own rights."

At its first session the legislative council addressed him in the most flattering terms, while the house of Representatives returned their thanks to him for his opening speech; using the following words:—"We discern the solicitude for the future happiness and prosperity of the territory, which has uniformly been evinced by your past administration."

Many other compliments were paid to MR. HARRISON, some of which we shall mention hereafter.

Governor HARRISON was surrounded by warlike tribes who were constantly fighting and quarrelling with the white settlers; while, as if to aggravate the troubles, hunters from Kentucky and Ohio were continually crossing into Indiana and destroying the game of right belonging to the Indians. The deer, bear and buffalo, were killed, merely for their skins; while the savages only took as many as were required for food. The Indians found their very living daily diminishing, with the prospect of soon being taken from them entirely by the promiscuous murder of the whites. Of this the savages complained most bitterly, and the Governor endeavored to prevent the incursions of the hunters.

To this was added the conduct of the British agents, who were continually prejudicing the minds of the Indians, and furnishing them with liquor. When Governor HARRISON would give notice for the meeting of a council, these agents would go immediately among the tribes and endeavor to inflame them against the United States. In November, 1804, Colonel M'KEE, the English agent used the following language to some of the chiefs:—"My children, it is true that the Americans do not wish you to drink any spiritous liquors, and therefore have told their traders that they should not carry any liquor into your country. But, my children, they have no right to say that one of your father's traders, (meaning the British traders,) should carry no liquor among his children.

"My children, your Father, King GEORGE, loves his red children, and wishes his red children supplied with every thing they want. He is not like the Americans, who are continually blinding your eyes, and stopping your ears with good words, that taste sweet as sugar, while they get all your lands from you."

By way of retaliation for the destruction of their game by the hunters, the Indians would kill the hogs and poultry of the settlers. The latter became incensed at this conduct, and frequently demanded to be led against the savages. With the general government insisting upon peace and forbearance, and the Indians inflamed by the British traders and committing constant depredations—the settlers suffering for the sins of the hunters, Governor HARRISON was placed in a most trying situation. It is only to be wondered that,—under all these circumstances and the course which naturally devolved upon him, and which he discharged so faithfully,—he preserved his popularity at all.

When the Indians came into a council, they frequently brought several hundred warriors, as if to intimidate the Governor; and they often behaved with so much insolence that he was obliged to send them away without effecting the objects of the meeting. They would come armed, and their orators would make the most inflammatory addresses to their warriors; yet the Governor was never known to betray the slightest fear. With but a handful of friends, would he meet hosts of these warlike and uncultivated savages—listen attentively to their appeals, and when the torrent of exciting native eloquence swelled to a dangerous height, with a calm dignity which never deserted him in his most perilous positions, he would with a few words spoken in a collected, though firm and decided tone, allay instantly the rude whirlwind of speech and bring down the uncouth savage from his flight of insolence and vituperation.

Often, when almost alone, he had peremptorally dismissed hundreds of Indians, burning for his blood, telling them, "They were disobedient children, and that he would listen to them no longer."

On one occasion, a plot was laid to assassinate him, but he was secretly informed of it just about the time that a council was to meet. He had but a few friends with him, and the Indians numbered over four hundred. Arming a small guard, all he could raise at the moment, he stationed them in a concealed position, and with his friends, went to the council. Upon a preconcerted signal, a chief suddenly started up and flourished his tomahawk to bury it in the head of the Governor. The latter rose at the same moment, and placing his hand gently upon the uplifted arm of the savage, spoke a few words very calmly, which induced the Indian to suppose that his plan had been betrayed, and that Governor HARRISON was fully prepared for any attempt that might be made upon him. "Be seated, my friend, be seated," said the Governor, in a tone of decision and authority. The chief stood amazed for a few moments, while the eye of the Governor was fixed upon his, and the tribes only waited the signal for a general melee. The spirit of the haughty savage was soon curbed, and apologizing for the assault, he resumed his seat and the business of the council proceeded.

Frequent attempts were made upon his life, but fortunately for his country they all proved abortive.

CHAPTER XII.

Notice of Ol-li-wa-chi-ca and Tecumthe—The religious principles of the Prophet, and league of the brothers, for a concentration of the tribes.

WE are now about to introduce to the reader two noted Indian characters, who began about the year 1806 to disturb the whole frontier. They were brothers; the one being a prophet, and the other a brave, daring, and sagacious warrior, an eloquent orator, and an able commander. We allude to OL-LI-WA-CHI-CA[4] and TECUMTHE. They are said, upon good authority to have been members of the Kishopoke tribe of the Shawanee nation.[5] These two, and still another—KUMSHAKA, were the offspring of the same mother at the same birth. They were born, it is generally allowed, on the banks of the Scioto, near Chilicothe. Their father, a great Shawanee warrior, fell at the battle of Kenhawa. Their mother was a Cherokee. She was taken prisoner by the Shawanees, and adopted agreeably to the Indian custom, by a family of that nation residing near the Miami of the Lakes. Hence some have considered her a Shawanee, while others supposed her to be a Creek. We put her down as a Cherokee, because TECUMTHE himself so informed a gentleman at Vincennes, and from the fact, that at an advanced age she migrated into the Cherokee country, and there died. KUMSHAKA is supposed to have died young, as he took no part with his brothers in their extensive operations.

---

[4] By some, we find the Prophet called Elskawatawa. Mr. Schoolcraft interprets this last to mean, "a fire that is moved from place to place." We also find his name written Olliwayshila, though not upon the best authority. Mr. Thatcher, in his Indian Biography, suggests that he may have assumed different names at different periods, and, from his character and pursuits, we are inclined to the same opinion. We adopt the one in the text as the name by which he is now generally designated.

[5] "Shawanee," among the Delawares, means, the "south;" and this tribe came originally from that section of the country. Mr. Heckewelder was informed by several old Mohicans, that the Shawanees formerly lived in the neighborhood of Savannah, in Georgia, and in the Floridas.

Some of the Shawanees have asserted, that TECUMTHE, at a very early age, was in an engagement with the Kentucky troops, and that he most ungallantly fled from the field, whilst his brother manfully stood his ground. Be that as it may, he never shrunk after. His cowardly conduct upon this occasion, is attributed to his extreme youth. By the time he was twenty-five, (about the year 1795,) he had acquired a great reputation among the Indians as a bold and fearless warrior. He intercepted more boats of the whites upon the Ohio, and plundered more houses of the settlers, than any Indian of his age. He was a perfect wasp among the Kentucky pioneers, who frequently pursued him but were never so fortunate as to overtake him. Upon such occasions, he would retreat to the banks of his favorite Wabash, until the storm was hushed; and when they were quietly returning to their domestic avocations, he would sweep like an overcharged torrent down upon the settlements. It is said that he never retained any of the plunder for himself, but gave all to his followers, satisfied with the glory of his achievements as his only reward. In these irruptions upon the border towns, he was but schooling himself for the grand scenes which he afterward planned, and to a certain extent executed.

The brothers conceived the project of uniting all the eastern tribes in a terrible war against the Americans. The two having evidently agreed upon a system of operations, OL-LI-WA-CHI-CA began in 1804, to inculcate among the Indians a *reformed* religion. In the course of his preaching it appears that he frequently changed the doctrines himself—those tenets that became unpopular among the disciples, were abandoned for more attractive and more fascinating principles. He began by explaining the inconsistency of the Indians in assuming the manners and dress of the whites—censured the introduction of spiritous liquors, and talked of the diseases, contentions and wars, produced by the contiguity of the residences of the white and red men. He showed the latter how fast their means of subsistence were diminishing, and how their territory was contracting daily. He then pictured to them the peaceful, happy, and contented lives of their forefathers.

Having by these appeals and declarations produced a feeling in his favor, he next went on to convince them of his own commission from the Great Spirit. In this he was obliged to bring others to his assistance, who vouched for the many wonderful miracles he had performed, and the benefits he was to confer on his followers.

The tribes were to unite, and not fight any longer with each other. They were to wear skins as their forefathers had done, and to use no ardent spirits. Stealing, quarrelling, and many minor crimes, were strictly prohibited. And then they were told, that if they adhered permanently to these doctrines, the Great Spirit would bless them, and they should be entirely separated from the whites and live in harmony among themselves.

The plan of the prophet was well calculated to make an impression upon the untutored savages, and was undoubtedly the suggestion of a strong and calculating mind. Some suppose that it originated entirely with OL-LI-WA-CHI-CA, but there is much reason to suppose that TECUMTHE had his share in drawing up the original plot. Others imagine that the two were directed and governed in their pursuits by the English, but when we consider the time at which the reformation, if we may so speak, begun; there is very little reason to conjecture that any others were concerned in the plan but the brothers themselves. The reformation was promulgated at a time when a general peace prevailed, which had been produced by the victories of the brave army of WAYNE; and though the British traders influenced the Indians against the Americans, they would scarcely have ventured to advise the organization of tens of thousands of red warriors in a general and indiscriminate contest against the whites.

The plan of uniting all the tribes against the whites was not however original with TECUMTHE and OL-LI-WA-CHI-CA. PONTIAC,[6] the Ottawa chief, many years before projected a similar concentration for the immediate extinction of the British, and so far succeeded in carrying out his views, that no less than nine English forts were captured by the Indians almost upon one day. We have also seen it stated that SAGUOAHA, the Keeper-Awake, or RED JACKET, as he was called by the whites, first gave to TECUMTHE the idea of a general combination; but from the character of that chief, and the part he took with the Americans, we do not place much reliance on this report.[7]

Toward the close of the life of this great Indian orator, the author frequently visited his residence, and at one time almost daily, and held familiar

---

[6] It has been stated by respectable authority, that this celebrated individual was a member of the tribe of Sacks or Sawxies; but there appears to us no sufficient reason for disputing the almost universal opinion which makes him an Ottawa.—Thatcher's Indian Biography.

[7] See Vol. II., of the work quoted in the above note.

intercourse with him. The only things which the good old chief appeared to regret as connected with the whites and Indians, were the sale of liquor to his people and the attempts of the clergy to draw him from the religion of his fathers.

For some years the success of the Prophet was quite doubtful, and his converts were few. His brother was, of course, the first to embrace the new fangled doctrine, and shortly after some of his relations and intimate friends embraced the tenets. He now gained a great influence over his own tribe, and flattered the pride of the SHAWANEEs by renewing an old tradition which made them the wisest, most intelligent, and respectable people in the world. This we give in the language of an old Shawanee chief, who spoke at the council at Fort Wayne, upon the subject, in 1803. Much of this speech was addressed directly to Governor HARRISON. With much native dignity, the venerable savage thus delivered himself:—

"The Master of Life who was himself an Indian, made the Shawanees before any others of the human race, and *they* sprang from his brain.[8] The Master of Life gave them all the knowledge which he himself possessed. He placed them upon the great island,[9] and all the other red people are descended from the Shawanees, he made the French and English out of his breast. The Dutch he made out of his feet. As for your Long Knives[10] kind, he made them out his hands. All those inferior races of men he made white, and placed them beyond the great lake.[11]

"The Shawanees were masters of the continent for many ages, using the knowledge which they had received from the Great Spirit, in such a manner as to be pleasing to him, and to secure their own happiness. In a great length of time however they became corrupt and the Master of Life told them he would take away from them the knowledge they possessed and give it to the white people; to be restored when, by a return to good principles, they would deserve it.

---

[8] There is a strong resemblance here to the mythological account of the creation of Minerva.

[9] The Continent of America.

[10] The Americans, though at first the term was applied by the Indians to the Virginians and Kentuckians.

[11] The Atlantic Ocean.

"Many years after that, they saw something white approaching their shores. At first they took it for a great bird, but they soon found it to be a monstrous canoe, filled with the very people who had got the knowledge which belonged to the Shawanees, but they usurped their lands also. They pretended, indeed, to have purchased their lands, but the very goods which they gave for them were more the property of the Indians than of the white people, because the knowledge which enabled them to manufacture these goods actually belonged to the Shawanees.

"But these things will now have an end. The Master of Life is about to restore to the Shawanees both their knowledge and their rights, and he will trample the Long Knives under his feet."

The old chief who delivered the above was supposed to be in the British interest, and that his object was to prevent all negotiations. The Prophet used the tradition, and by it brought over thousands to his way of thinking. The subject was a good one, and he turned it at once to his own purpose.

CHAPTER XIII.

Notice of the Prophet—Tanner's account—Murder of the chiefs—Anecdote of the Dead Chief.—The Prophet's message to Governor Harrison—The latter's conduct to the Indians—The Prophet visits the Governor at Vincennes.

THE success of an Indian Prophet depends principally upon his skill in deception, and OL-LI-WA-CHI-CA had all the necessary cunning for beginning his career, though he does not seem to have possessed sufficient penetration for conducting operations after they had swelled to importance. Tanner says that while he was living at Great Wood River, a stranger from the Shawanees visited that section of the country for the purpose of making proselytes. He told the Indians that they should not let the fire go out in their lodges—that they should not let their dogs live—they should not strike a man, woman, child or dog—they should not drink, steal, lie, or go against their enemies, and that they must not use flint or steel. Most of the Indians complied with all these injunctions, but TANNER for a long time refused. "The Ojibbeway whom I have mentioned," he continued, "remained sometime among the Indians in my neighborhood, and gained the attention of the principal men so effectually, that a time was appointed, and a lodge prepared for the solemn and public espousing of the doctrines of the Prophet. When the people, and I among them, were brought into the lodge, prepared for this solemnity, we saw something carefully concealed under a blanket, in figure and dimensions bearing some strong resemblance to the form of a man."

"Four strings of mouldy and discolored beans were all the remaining visible insignia of this important mission. After a long harangue, in which the prominent features of the new revelation were stated and urged upon the attention of all, the four strings of beans, which we were told were made of the flesh itself of the Prophet, were carried with much solemnity, to each man in the lodge, and he was expected to take hold of each string at the top, and draw them gently through his hands. This was called shaking hands with the

Prophet, and was considered as solemnly engaging to obey his injunctions, and accept his mission as from the Supreme."

It was a long time before TANNER would kill his dogs and give up his medicine bag, but at last he gave way with the rest and followed many, though not all, of the instructions of the Prophet. The latter was opposed by many of the chiefs, and these he accused of witchcraft, and had them murdered by their own people. TETEBOXTI, a Delaware chief, eighty years of age, was condemned to the stake, but when the fire was about to be kindled, a young Indian stepped from the crowd; and with his tomahawk, put an end to the old man's existence.

BILLY PATTERSON, an Indian who had resided many years among the whites, was condemned to a similar death; and died with a hymn book in his hand, singing and praying until his voice was hushed by the flames.

SHATEYARONRAH, or LEATHER-LIPS, a Wyandot chief, was ordered to be murdered. The messengers found the old warrior, and they commenced digging his grave by the side of his wigwam. Finding entreaty vain, he dressed himself in his best war clothes—took a meal of venison, and knelt at the edge of his grave. He and his executioner prayed together. The Indians withdrew to a short distance, and seated themselves on the ground. "The old chief inclined forward, resting his face upon his hand, and his hand upon his knees. While thus seated, one of the young Indians came up and struck him twice with the tomahawk. For some time he lay senseless upon the ground, the only remaining evidence of life being a faint respiration. The Indians all stood around in solemn silence. Finding him to breathe longer than they expected, they called upon the whites (one or two of whom were spectators,) to take notice how hard he died; pronounced him a wizard,—'no good,'—then struck him again, and terminated his existence."[12]

These statements exhibit the great influence which OL-LI-WA-CHI-CA obtained over the western tribes. He took care to remove all the prominent men who were opposed to him, while his brother was actively engaged in stirring up the Indians to rise at once upon the American settlements. TECUMTHE made repeated tours among the tribes, almost from one end of the continent to the other. He was received with respect wherever he went,

---

[12] See Thatcher's Indian Biography.

und listened to with attention. He pictured to the councils the happiness of their ancestors, and compared their extensive possessions and unlimited enjoyments, with the present scarcity of game and contracted territory. He spoke of the warlike and independent character of their fathers, and exhibited their own pusillanimity and degraded condition. The noble, free and upright habits of the one were compared with the profligacy, corruption and drunkenness of the other. Some he threatened; others he persuaded. There was no argument which native intelligence could suggest, that he did not use to accomplish his design; and to rivet whatever hold his reasoning might have gained with his auditory, he boldly asserted that OL-LI-WA-CHI-CA could prevent the bullets of the enemy from taking effect upon the body of an Indian;—that he himself would fearlessly lead the attack, and they should see him rush unharmed into the thickest of the foe.

The brothers even went so far as, (at one time,) to propose the murder of all the leading chiefs who had ever signed any treaties with the United States, by which any territory was relinquished; and some of the old Winnebago chiefs declared to an American scout, with tears in their eyes, that they had no longer any power over their people, every thing being managed exclusively by the warriors. To show still more forcibly the character of TECUMTHE, we will give an anecdote from DAWSON's Memoirs of Harrison. At a conference held at Vincennes, TECUMTHE was present, and so also, a noted Potawatamie, called the DEAD CHIEF, because he was deaf TECUMTHE, on that occasion, being charged by Governor HARRISON with hostile intentions against the Americans, he disclaimed the accusation. The next day the DEAD CHIEF called upon Governor HARRISON, and asked, why *he* had not been required to confront TECUMTHE. He said he would have willingly asserted the truth before all the Indians. The Shawanee having heard this, gave word to his brother to have the DEAD CHIEF despatched. The latter hearing of this, put on his war dress, painted himself, took his arms, and at once paddled his canoe directly to the camp of TECUMTHE. MR. BARON, the Governor's interpreter, was in the tent of the Shawanee at the time the DEAD CHIEF arrived. The latter upbraided TECUMTHE for having given the order to have him assassinated— told him it was cowardly and unworthy a warrior. "But here I am:—come and kill me!" cried the old Indian. "You and your men can kill the white people's hogs, and call them bears, but you cannot face a warrior." He then went on to insult and provoke Tecumthe; called him the slave of the English, and a base dog. "During the whole time Tecumthe seemed not in the least to regard him, but continued to converse with Mr. Baron. Wearied at length with his useless efforts to draw out his adversary, he gave the war-whoop of defiance, and paddled off in his canoe. "There is reason," adds Mr. Dawson, "to believe that the order of Tecumthe was obeyed. *The Dead Chief was no more seen at Vincennes.*"

During the year 1807, intelligence reached Governor Harrison of the movements of the savages, and particularly of the conduct of Ol-li-wa-chi-ca toward the chiefs of the various tribes. The Governor immediately sent a message to the Shawanees noticing their measures, and reprehending them in the severest terms. He told the chiefs they were listening "to a fool that speaks not the words of the Great Spirit, but the words of the devil." Most of the chiefs being absent, the Prophet dictated to the messenger the following reply to the Governor:—

"Father:

"I am sorry that you listen to the advice of bad birds. You have impeached me with having correspondence with the English, and with calling and sending for the Indians from the most distant parts of the country, 'to listen to a fool that speaks not the words of the Great Spirit, but the words of the devil.'

"Father! These impeachments I deny, and say they are not true. I never had a word with the English, and I never sent for any Indians. They came here themselves, to listen and hear the words of the Great Spirit.

"Father! I wish you would not listen any more to the voice of bad birds; and you may rest assured that it is the least of our ideas to make disturbance; and we will rather try to stop such proceedings than encourage them."

In the spring of 1808, great numbers of Indians were in the vicinity of Fort Wayne. They had neglected their corn fields to listen to the Prophet, and were almost in a state of starvation. To prevent incursions upon the settlements, the Governor wisely ordered the agent at Fort Wayne to supply them with provisions from the public stores. Toward the beginning of summer, the Prophet selected a spot on the upper part of the Wabash, called Tippecanoe, as his future and permanent residence. Thither he removed, and his disciples followed him.

In July he sent word to the Governor that he was coming to see him, for the purpose of explaining how grossly he had been misrepresented. The next month he arrived at Vincennes, where he remained for two weeks. While here, he denied being in the British interest, and asserted that his sole object was to reclaim the Indians from their bad habits, and cause them to live in peace with all mankind. He frequently addressed his disciples in presence of the Governor, and spoke constantly of the evils of war and spiritous liquors.

When leaving Vincennes, he addressed the Governor, and declared that he did not wish the Indians to take up the tomahawk, either for the British or the Long Knives.

In his address to the Legislature, in 1809, the Governor mentions the conduct of the Prophet, who had become dissatisfied with the treaty made at Fort Wayne, in the autumn of the preceding year. The Governor sent word to the Prophet, that he might come forward and exhibit any title he might have to the land transferred by the treaty, and if it was "found to be just and equitable, the lands would be restored, or an ample equivalent given for them." His brother met Governor HARRISON, and claimed the land, because he said they belonged to all the tribes, and could not be parted with except by consent of all. This argument was too absurd to command any attention, and TECUMTHE returned to the Wabash, in no very good humor. He now redoubled his exertions for the concentration of all the western tribes, but was extremely guarded in his efforts, to prevent the Governor from receiving any intimation of his proceedings.

CHAPTER XIV.

Tecumthe visits Governor Harrison at Vincennes—His conduct—Speech—The Governor's reply—Tecumthe's insolence—He is dismissed—The Governor visits Tecumthe at his camp—The latter goes to the south.

THE Governor sent word to TECUMTHE not to bring more than thirty warriors with him to Vincennes in the summer of 1810, but he came with over three hundred, all completely armed. This numerous body guard created an unusual sensation in the town, and many supposed that the savages were about to commence a general war on the instant. The haughty chief gave as an excuse for this armed escort, that he believed there was treachery intended on the part of the whites. Seats were prepared in a large portico in front of the Governor's residence, but when TECUMTHE came from his camp with about forty warriors, he refused to enter the portico, and requested that the council might be held under the shade of a cluster of trees in front of the house.

When the trouble of moving the seats was mentioned, he said it would only be "necessary to remove those intended for the whites. The red men are accustomed to sit upon the earth which is their mother, and we are always happy to recline upon her bosom." This occurred on the 12th of August, and TECUMTHE then delivered the following speech:—

"What I am I have become by my own exertions; and I would that I could make the red men as great as I picture them in my mind, when I think of the Great Spirit, and his wish to render all his people noble and happy. Were such the case I would not come to General HARRISON beseeching him to annul the treaty; but I would say to him, 'Brother, you are at liberty to return to your own country.' There was a time when the foot of the white man did not crush the fallen limbs in our paths. This country then belonged to all the red men. It was created for the red man and his children. We were all united, and the Great Spirit placed us here, and filled the land with fruit and game for our use. We were then happy. We are now made miserable by the white man, who is never contented, but asks us for more and more land. The white people have driven us from the great salt lake. They follow us over the mountains as we retire to the setting sun. They would force us into the lakes, but we are determined to go no further.

"The march of the white man must be stopped. The Indians must insist upon the original compact. The land belongs to all, and all must still own it. It was our fathers. We must give it to our children. It cannot be divided.

"We have no right to sell, even to each other. How then can we sell it to strangers? Why should we, when they are never satisfied? The land is ours, and the white men have no right to take it from us. The Indians should they sell, can only do so when all the tribes are together, and when all consent. No sale is valid unless made by all. The late sale was made only by a few tribes, and it is therefore nugatory."

In his reply, Governor HARRISON said, that "when the white people arrived on this continent, they found the Miamies in the occupation of all the country in the Wabash, and at that time the Shawanees were residents of Georgia, from which they were driven by the Creeks. The lands have been purchased from the Miamies, who were the true and original owners of it. It is ridiculous to assert that all the Indians are one nation, for if such had been the intention of the Great Spirit, he would not have put six different tongues into their heads, but would have taught them all to speak one language.

"The Miamies have found it to their interest to sell a part of their lands, and to receive for them a further annuity, in addition to what they have long enjoyed; and the benefit of which they have experienced from the punctuality with which the seventeen fires[13] comply with their engagements: and the Shawanees have no right to come from a distant country to control the Miamies in the disposal of their own property."

The interpreter had no sooner finished, than TECUMTHE bounded from the earth and cried, "It is false!" He gave a signal to his band, and every man leaped up, and seized his war club. The Governor was only attended by a few unarmed citizens, and his situation was now extremely perilous. The Governor's honorary guard of twelve soldiers, had been directed to occupy a shady place at some distance from the council. Retaining that admirable command over himself which never deserted him even under the most

---

[13] The seventeen United States.

dangerous circumstances, the Governor laid his hand upon his sword, and directed his friends and suite to stand upon their guard. TECUMTHE addressed the Indians in a loud and fierce tone, and with impetuous gesticulation. WINNEMAK, a friendly chief, cocked a pistol; Major FLOYD drew his dirk, and a Methodist minister, named WINANS, ran to the residence of the Governor, seized a rifle, and prepared to protect the family. The action of the Indians appeared preconcerted, and all expected a fierce and daring assault. The guard approached with their pieces levelled, and would have fired had they not been checked by the Governor.

After waiting a few moments to see what course the savages would pursue, the Governor said to TECUMTHE, in a calm, but firm and decided tone, that "he was a bad man—that he would have no further talk with him—that he must return now to his camp, and take his departure from the settlements immediately."

It is said by those who were present, that had the Governor betrayed the least fear or surprise, TECUMTHE would have given the signal for a general assault. There are good reasons for supposing that such was his real intention, but the authoritative manner of his antagonist completely subdued the savage; and finding he could not intimidate, he called off his warriors and returned quietly to his encampment.

The next morning the haughty chief apologized for the insult, and desired that the council might be renewed. To this the Governor consented, taking the precaution to have two companies of militia under arms, to protect Vincennes. At this second meeting TECUMTHE denied the intention of an attack, but said that he had been advised to the course he had pursued by two white men who had visited his residence a short time previous, and who told him that the people were opposed to the Governor, and were willing to give back the land. At this interview, the chief conducted himself with perfect respect toward the Governor, but still insisted upon the arguments he had urged the previous day. He said he was determined to insist upon the *old boundary*. He was openly supported in this resolution by several chiefs of five different tribes. The council ended by the Governor telling him that his words should be reported to the President.

Still anxious to reconcile TECUMTHE, the Governor visited him the next day at his own camp. The chief had by this time been taught to respect his guest, and his proud spirit bent before his superior. Mr. Harrison was received with kindness and the most polite attention. Almost alone, he went in among many hundreds of rude warriors, but Tecumthe well knew that he must respect a man possessed of such true courage. He himself had been afraid to venture with forty warriors, to the Governor's house. The Governor was now in Tecumthe's shantee with but half a dozen attendants.

They remained together for a long time, but the chief still adhered to all his previous grounds, with the most provoking obstinacy, and when the Governor told him that he felt confident the President would not agree to his proposals, he haughtily replied:—

"Well, as the great chief is to determine the matter, I hope the Great Spirit will put sense enough in his head to induce him to direct you to give up this land. It is true, he is so far off that he will not be injured by the war. He may sit still in his town, and drink his wine, while you and I have to fight it out."

Soon after this Tecumthe withdrew to the Prophet's town, and a trader in whom Governor Harrison had the utmost confidence, reported that the Prophet had at least a thousand souls under his control. But a few months more had passed, when further information reached Vincennes, that nearly one thousand warriors were assembled at Tippecanoe—many of them from the northern tribes—and that a general combination was openly talked of. The Governor immediately sent for a leading member of the Shaker Society, (who had asserted that the Prophet was almost as good a Shaker as he was himself,) and endeavoured to prevail upon him to take a message to the prophet.

In this message the Governor pictured the disastrous consequences of a general war, and used the following expression:—"Brothers! I am myself of the Long Knife fire. As soon as they hear my voice, you will see them pouring forth their swarms of hunting-shirt men, as numerous as the mosquitoes on the shores of the Wabash. Brothers! take care of their stings."

In answer to this, Tecumthe sent word that he would meet the Governor in eighteen days, "to wash away all those bad stories." He arrived on the 27th of July, 1811, with three hundred men. At the council he appeared with two hundred warriors all armed, while the Governor was at the head of a full troop of dragoons, armed but dismounted. A rain coming on, the meeting adjourned to the next day, when the business proceeded.

The Governor demanded that two Potawatamie murderers who were at Tippecanoe, should be given up. "It is not right," said TECUMTHE, "to punish these people. They ought to be forgiven, as well as those who have recently murdered my people at the Illinois. The whites should follow my example in forgiving; I have forgiven the Ottawas and the Osages." He wished matters to remain as they were, until he could return from a visit which he was about to make to the southern Indians; then, he said, he would go to Washington himself, and settle all their difficulties with the President. "In the meanwhile," he said, "I will despatch messengers to all the neighboring tribes, (who are wholly under my control,) to prevent further mischief."

When he had concluded, he offered the Governor a quantity of wampum in atonement for the murders. The present was refused with an indignant reply, and the council broke up. TECUMTHE returned to Tippecanoe, and shortly after, attended by only a few followers, commenced his journey to the south.

CHAPTER XV.

Conduct of the Prophet—Gathering of the Indians at Tippecanoe—The Governor receives orders to march against the Indians—Volunteers flock to his standard—March of the army. Great skill of the commander in choosing routes, crossing Pine Creek, &c.

THE Prophet's town was the grand centre for all the Indians, and TECUMTHE was careful, wherever he found them willing to engage in the combination, to send them at once to his brother. Here they were not allowed to retrograde in their determination, for they were surrounded by hundreds gathered from various tribes, all collected for the same purpose, and constantly harangued by the Prophet, who touched every chord to rouse their feelings, and fed them with new themes to excite their superstitions. He practised awful incantations, and revived many of the ancient rites of the Indians. He indulged the spirit of prophecy to its fullest extent, and told his followers of hundreds of charms which he could give to protect them from the weapons of the white man.

Having duped his followers into a conviction that he could do all he said, he encouraged them to make assaults upon the more exposed settlements. Houses were robbed, horses stolen—and soon, even murders were committed. His encampment was daily filling up with the bold and daring of even the most distant tribes, and his force soon amounted to more than one thousand warriors.

Called together for the express purpose of attacking the whites, they became restless and uneasy. Their savage habits could bear no restraint, nor did the Prophet attempt to control them in their lawless desires. Parties roved about the country, and scarcely rose the sun but his rays fell upon the mangled bodies of helpless women and children, and the smoking ruins of the settler's cabin.

These outrages could no longer be borne, and Governor HARRISON proceeded to place the territory in as defensible a position as its limited resources would allow. At his own earnest solicitation, and the repeated petitions of the people, in 1811, he received directions from the President to march against the Prophet's town with an armed force. He was, however, commanded peremptorily to avoid hostilities "of any kind, or to any degree, not indispensably required."

The news of the Governor's authority to march against the Indians, was received with rapture through the whole west, particularly in Kentucky, where it was met with joy and delight.

The people had suffered so long—the country had been so completely overrun by the savages, and so many barbarities had been practised upon the settlers, that they burned for revenge, and in crowds volunteered their services for the dangerous expedition. The people knew their commander to be brave, patriotic and skilful, and many of the first men in the country flocked eagerly to his standard. General SAMUEL WELLS, previously distinguished in similar service—Colonel ABRAHAM OWEN, a veteran in Indian warfare—JOSEPH H. DAVIESS, an eminent lawyer, rushed to the side of the intrepid HARRISON. Colonel GUIGER raised a small company of young men near Louisville, and joined the gallant leader. CROGHAN, O'FALLON, EDWARDS, SHIPP, and CHEEM, afterward distinguished officers of our army, were among the brave men who came to HARRISON's assistance. Colonel BOYD's regiment, the fourth United States Infantry, was, at his request, placed under the command of the western hero.

The army numbered a little over nine hundred, but they were gallant men, determined to do or die. Three hundred and fifty were infantry of the regular service. The rest were volunteer militia from Indiana, excepting sixty or seventy men from Kentucky. One hundred and twenty were dragoons. We have already described the mode of formation introduced by WAYNE, and so successfully practised in 1794;—Governor HARRISON immediately commenced instructing his soldiers in the same manner.

The army commenced its march from Fort Harrison, a post on the Wabash about sixty miles above Vincennes, on the 28th of October. Application was made to the Prophet, through the Delaware and Miami Indians, for the surrender of the two Potawatamie murderers alluded to in the speech of TECUMTHE, in the preceding chapter; and also for the return of a number of horses which had been stolen from the whites. The demand was treated with contempt, and the envoys with insolence. The Prophet even went so far as to send off a war party, with directions to massacre any white men they might find. They advanced so near upon the army as to fire upon the sentinel. The brothers had their plans so far prepared, that OL-LI-WA-CHI-CA thought it was no longer necessary even to pretend friendship with the United States; and though his brother was absent, he thought his position sufficiently safe to resist any force that could at that time be brought against him.

The American troops on their march to Tippecanoe, were encamped in the order of battle; and moved so that they would form for action almost instantly. The infantry marched in two columns, single file, while the cavalry and mounted riflemen, covered the advance, flank and rear. Thus by a single evolution, the army could present two lines to receive the enemy at any point, or form a hollow square. The dragoons and riflemen changed positions as the ground varied, so that they were kept where it was best adapted to their respective modes of fighting.

Five friendly Indians and a Frenchman eating as scouts were kept out constantly, and advanced guards to protect the main body from savage ambuscade. The situation of the commander was a trying one—a horde of blood-thirsty Indians in advance; prepared for war and led by a skilful chief; numerous and widely scattered settlements in his rear, dependent upon him for protection. Although MR. EUSTIS, the secretary of war, had written to him, "The banditti under the Prophet are to be attacked and vanquished;" yet he immediately added "provided such a measure shall be deemed *absolutely* necessary;" and from the moderate tone of the order, the commander was to fight when attacked and not before. Thus the enemy had the choice of time, place and manner; while Governor HARRISON could only take precautionary measures.

Just beyond Fort Harrison two routes were presented. Causing a road to be made on the south side of the Wabash, the army advanced upon it a short distance, when by an admirable movement, the Governor threw his whole force across the river, and marched over wide plains where there was but little opportunity for a secret attack. By this manœuvre the plans of the Indians were totally frustrated, and for three days no sign of an enemy was seen.

For several days the scouts had not been in, and it was uncertain whether the Indians had passed the army with the view of attacking the settlements, or had retired to Tippecanoe. The towns were much exposed, particularly Vincennes, which at that time was the most westerly. The idea of an attack upon this place so distressed the Governor as to drive from him his accustomed slumber. He arose in the night and having sent for Major JORDON, of the Indiana volunteers, directed him to take forty picked men, and proceed at once back to Vincennes, to protect that post, and place it and other exposed settlements, upon their guard. In case of any disaster to the army, he was to fortify the court house, and such other buildings as could be defended—remove the women and children into them, and send expresses to the Governor of Kentucky, inviting volunteers.

By Major JORDON the Governor wrote to his friend, DR. SCOTT, (who was at Vincennes to attend Mrs. Harrison in an expected indisposition) that his only uneasiness was for the wives and children of himself and his brave companions. That he had no fears for the success of the campaign. That he was aware that he was much exposed, because nearly all the Indians knew his person and were hostile to him. That his life was in the hands of his Creator, and DR. SCOTT might rest assured that he would bring no disgrace upon the character of a pupil of WAYNE. Should he fall he recommended his family to the care of his friend.[14]

Major JORDON performed the duty intrusted to him, though he expressed much reluctance in being called from that which promised to be more active service. November 4th, the army arrived at Pine creek, and prepared to cross its difficult pass. The course of the stream for many miles above its confluence with the Wabash, is through a deep channel, among immense rocks, forming frequent and perpendicular precipices. The crossings are few, and through

---

[14] Dr. Scott, the gentleman to whom this letter was addressed, afterwards commanded the first regiment of Kentucky volunteers under General Harrison. His regiment composed a part of the detachment ordered by the General from Fort Wayne, to destroy the Potawatamie town at Elk Hart. Being in bad health, the General desired him not to accompany the detachment, assuring him that there would be no fighting, as the Indians could not assemble in that quarter in time to make head against the detachment. In despite of these remonstrances, the gallant Colonel appeared at the head of his regiment, and declared that no other person should lead it towards the enemy, while he was able to mount his horse. The service was effected without opposition; but the patriotic Colonel was taken sick upon his return, and shortly afterwards expired, a victim to his high sense of military etiquette.—Note by Judge Hall, in his Memoirs of Harrison.

narrow defiles; so that the regular order of the army must be broken, and open to ambuscades. In 1786 and 1790, American troops had been surprised on this very spot. A like danger to the present expedition was prevented by the consummate skill of the Governor, who suddenly quitted the usual path, and passed the creek at another place, which he had ordered to be surveyed the previous night.

In this march the Governor displayed that superior tact for which he has always been remarkable. By crossing the Wabash directly after leaving Fort Harrison, he completely deceived the enemy. By choosing a new spot where to cross Pine creek, he effectually frustrated any secret design his foe might have formed, and was in the heart of the enemy's country and in front of his town, almost before the Indians knew of his march.

CHAPTER XVI.

March of the army—The Governor's conduct and care—A flag sent forward—The messenger insulted—The encampment—Battle of Tippecanoe.

ON the evening of the 5th of November, the army encamped within nine or ten miles of Tippecanoe, and the march upon the day following was conducted with the greatest caution, to avoid a surprise. About midday, the Indians began to show themselves, and to make insulting gestures to the soldiers. The interpreters called to them, but they would not listen. Having reached a favorable spot for an encampment, within a mile and a half of the town, the Governor determined to remain there and fortify his position until he could hear from the friendly Indians whom he had despatched from Fort Harrison, with a message to the Prophet, the day he left that place. He had as yet received no intelligence from them. While he was making a survey Major DAVIESS and several other officers, urged an immediate attack upon the town. It was represented to him that the Indians only threatened and insulted the interpreters—that their evident intention was to fight—that the troops were in excellent spirits and full of confidence, and that the present was the time to march. To this the Governor replied, that he still expected to hear from the friendly Indians—that he knew the spirit of the troops, and that however determined the Indians might be for a fight, they would never do so unless all things were in their favor. He was therefore determined not to advance, until he knew precisely the situation of the town, and the character of the ground around it, and between it and the camp. He said it was his duty to take care that they should not engage in a situation where their valor would be useless. That at present, a corps upon which he placed great reliance would be unable to act—that "the experience of the last two hours ought to convince every officer, that no reliance should be placed upon the guides, as to the topography of the country—that, relying on their information, the troops had been led into a situation so unfavorable, that but for the celerity with which they changed their position, a few Indians might have destroyed them: he was therefore determined not to advance to the town, until he had previously reconnoitered, either in person, or by some one on whose judgment he could rely." Major DAVIESS stated that he and his adjutant had surveyed the country and he described it to the Governor. The latter now determined to advance, and Captain T. DUBOIS offered his services to carry a flag. The Captain started forward with an interpreter, and the army moved slowly after, in order of battle.

The gallant envoy had not been gone long before he sent back a messenger to say that the Indians were around him in considerable numbers, and endeavoring to cut him off from the army; and that they would not listen to the interpreter. The Governor immediately recalled the Captain, and resolving to treat the Indians as enemies, moved on to attack them. He was met directly after by three Indians, one a counsellor of the Prophet. They were sent to know why the army was advancing upon them, and stated that the Prophet wished to avoid hostilities, and had sent a pacific message by the Indians despatched by the Governor from Fort Harrison, but that these men had unfortunately taken the southern route in their return, and thus missed the army. A suspension of hostilities was agreed upon, with the understanding that a council should be held the next day, to agree on terms of peace, the Governor informing the Indians that he would go on to the Wabash, and there encamp for the night. The Governor soon came in sight of the town, which stood on a commanding eminence at some distance up the river. Major DAVIESS mistook some scattering houses for the town itself. The army was still upon the march, the country below the town being unfavorable for an encampment; and such was the order, that by a single conversion of companies, all were ready for battle. A change of position being directed in consequence of the dragoons having become entangled in underwood, the Indians supposed their town was to be attacked, and they prepared to defend it. The Governor rode forward himself, and calling some Indians to him, told them that he had no intention of attacking them, but that he was seeking a proper location for an encampment, and for that purpose was going above the town. One of the savages acquainted with the Governor, told him that the creek they had crossed below, led to the north of the town, running through the prairie, and two officers were despatched to examine the spot. These soon returned, and reported that they had found an elevated situation, with plenty of fuel and water.

"An idea was propagated by the enemies of Harrison," says McAffee, "after the battle of Tippecanoe, that the Indians had forced him to encamp on a place chosen by them as suitable for the attack they intended. The place, however, was chosen, by Majors Taylor and Clarke, after examining all the environs of the town; and when the army of General Hopkins was there in the following year, they all united in the opinion that a better spot to resist Indians was not to be found in the whole country.

"The army now marched to the place selected, and encamped, late in the evening, on a dry piece of ground which rose about ten feet above the level of a marshy prairie in front towards the town, and about twice as high above a similar prairie in the rear; through which, near the bank, ran a small stream clothed with willows and brushwood. On the left of the encampment, this bench of land became wider; on the right it gradually narrowed, and terminated in an abrupt point, about one hundred and fifty yards from the right flank. The two columns of infantry occupied the front and rear. The right flank being about eight yards wide, was filled with Captain Spencer's company of eighty men. The left flank, about one hundred and fifty yards in extent, was composed of three companies of mounted riflemen, under General Wells, commanding as Major."

The place selected for the encampment was about three fourths of a mile, from Tippecanoe. The front line was formed by Major Floyd's U. S. infantry, and Colonel Bartholomew's Indiana militia. The rear was composed of Captain Baen's U. S. infantry, and Lieutenant Colonel Decker's Indiana volunteers. Spencer's men were volunteer riflemen from Indiana. General Wells' command consisted of Robb's company of Indiana volunteers and Guiger's company of volunteers, part from the latter territory, and part from Kentucky. A part of the government troops covered the left front and rear angles. Major Daviess' reserve cavalry were stationed in the rear of the left flank of the front line. The following description we give from McAffee, the author already quoted.

"The order given to the army, in the event of a night attack, was for each corps to maintain its ground at all hazards till relieved. The dragoons were directed in such case to parade dismounted, with their swords on and their pistols in their belts, and to wait for orders. The guard for the night consisted of two captains' commands of twenty-four men and four non-commissioned officers; and two subalterns' guards of twenty men and non-commissioned officers—the whole under the command of a field officer of the day.

"On the night of the 6th of November, the troops went to rest, as usual, with their clothes and accoutrements on, and their arms by their sides. The officers were ordered to sleep in the same manner, and it was the Governor's invariable practice to be ready to mount his horse at a moment's warning. On the morning of the 7th, he arose at a quarter before 4 o'clock, and sat by the fire conversing with the gentlemen of his family, who were reclining on their blankets waiting for the signal, which in a few minutes would have been given, for the troops to turn out. The orderly drum had already been roused for the reveille. The moon had risen, but afforded little light, in consequence of being overshadowed by clouds, which occasionally discharged a drizzling rain. At this moment the attack commenced.[15]

"The treacherous Indians had crept up so near the sentries as to hear them challenge when relieved. They intended to rush upon the sentries and kill them before they could fire; but one of them discovered an Indian creeping towards him in the grass, and fired. This was immediately followed by the Indian yell, and a desperate charge upon the left flank. The guard in that quarter gave way, and abandoned their officer without making any resistance. Captain BARTON's company of regulars, and Captain GUIGER's company of mounted riflemen, forming the left angle of the rear line, received the first onset. The fire there was excessive; but the troops who had lain on their arms, were immediately prepared to receive, and had gallantry to resist the furious savage assailants.

"The manner of the attack was calculated to discourage and terrify the men; yet as soon as they could be formed and posted, they maintained their ground with desperate valor, though but few of them had ever before been in

---

[15] Upon the first alarm the Governor mounted his horse, and proceeded towards the point of attack; and finding the line much weakened there, he ordered two companies from the centre of the rear line to march up, and form across the angle in the rear of Barton's and Guiger's companies. In passing through the camp towards the left of the front line, he met with Major Daviess, who informed him that the Indians, concealed behind some trees near the line, were annoying the troops very severely in that quarter, and requested permission to dislodge them. In attempting this exploit he fell mortally wounded, as did Colonel Isaac White of Indiana, who acted as a volunteer in his troop.—Judge Hall.

battle. The fires of the camp were extinguished immediately, as the light they afforded was more serviceable to the Indians than to our men."[16]

"In the mean time the attack on Spencer's and Warwick's companies, on the right, became very severe. Captain Spencer and his lieutenants were all killed, and Captain Warwick was mortally wounded. The Governor, in passing towards that flank, found Captain ROBB's company near the centre of the camp. They had been driven from their post; or rather, had fallen back without orders. He led them to the aid of Captain SPENCER, where they fought very bravely, having seventeen men killed during the battle. While the Governor was leading this company into action, Colonel OWEN, his aid, was killed at his side. This gallant officer was mounted on a white horse, and as the Governor had ridden a grey on the day before, it is probable that OWEN was mistaken for him, as it is certain that he was killed by one of the only Indians who broke through the lines, and who are supposed to have resolved to sacrifice themselves in an attempt to insure victory by killing the commander-in-chief. The Governor happened not to be mounted on his own grey; his servant had accidentally tied that animal apart from the other horses belonging to the general staff, and in the confusion occasioned by the attack, not being able to find this horse as quickly as was desirable, the Governor mounted another.

"Captain PRESCOTT's company of U. S. infantry had filled up the vacancy caused by the retreat of ROBB's company. Soon after DAVIESS was wounded, Captain SNELLING, by order of the Governor, charged upon the same Indians, and dislodged them with considerable loss. The battle was now maintained on all sides with desperate valor. The Indians advanced and retreated by a rattling noise made with deer hoofs; they fought with enthusiasm and seemed determined on victory or death."

As soon as it was daylight, the companies of SNELLING, POSEY, SCOTT and WILSON, were taken from the rear and formed on the left flank, and those of COOK and BAEN were ordered to the right. General WELLS was directed to command the corps on the left, and with the aid of some dragoons, who were now mounted, to charge the enemy in that direction. The service was gallantly performed, and the Indians were driven into a swamp, where the cavalry could

---

[16] Except those of Barton's and Guiger's companies, which the suddenness of the attack left no time to put out.—Hall.

not follow. "At the same time," says MCAFFEE, "COOK's and Lieutenant LARRABE's companies, with the aid of the riflemen and militia on the right flank, charged the Indians and put them to flight in that quarter, which terminated the battle."

CHAPTER XVII.

Governor Harrison's conduct at the Battle of Tippecanoe—His danger and his courage—Testimony of a private—Resolution of the Kentucky Legislature—Same of Indiana Legislature—Testimony of the militia—Opinion of President Madison—Trial and condemnation of the negro—His pardon—Governor Harrison's letter on the subject—Movements of Tecumthe and the Prophet—Return of the troops to Vincennes.

So much has been said about the celebrated and gallant action recorded in the preceeding chapter, that we do not feel disposed to allow the subject to pass from our hands without a few brief remarks upon the conduct of the distinguished commander. We feel more particularly called upon so to do, from the fact, that since we have been engaged upon this work, it has been stated to a friend of the author, by a gentleman who ought to have been better acquainted with the history of his country, that "General HARRISON *ran away* at the battle of Tippecanoe!"

Let us recapitulate a few facts for the benefit of the person alluded to, and all others who are wilfully ignorant of the leading events of the history of their own land. Governor HARRISON mounted a horse upon the first tap of the drum. The army encamped in order of battle, the commander himself having appointed the various positions of the troops. So anxious was he to act at once, that he mounted the first horse that came in his way, without waiting for his groom to bring his own charger. In the midst of the action, finding that the men were giving way in a particular part of the field, he himself headed two companies, and marched them into the very thickest of the fire. In leading this force, his aid was shot from his horse, by his side; and the Governor received a ball through the rim of his hat, at the same moment. He still led the two companies forward, and so destructive was the fire that from only one of those companies, seventeen men fell dead upon the field. Such was his conduct. Let us now go back a few years and examine his danger. He had been upon the frontier more than seventeen years, during the whole of which time he was in constant—almost daily intercourse with the savages. The leading men from nearly all the western tribes, had met him in council, and his person was known to them. Frequent attempts had been made to assassinate him, and the Indians thought if they could but put him out of the way, they might easily overcome the whole army. Men had been picked out for the express purpose of murdering him, and only the night before the action a negro was arrested, who was lurking near the Governor's marquee with the intention of killing him in his sleep. At the time of the action, this fellow was a prisoner in the camp.—To Governor HARRISON's courage we have the testimony of all the soldiers, officers and privates who ever served with him.

In a small work published at Keene, New Hampshire, as long ago as 1816, entitled, "A Journal of two campaigns of the Fourth Regiment of United States Infantry, by Adam Walker, a private in the 4th Regiment," the name of HARRISON is frequently mentioned in terms of the warmest admiration. It is not probable that the Governor ever knew the author, yet the latter undoubtedly speaks the views of all the common soldiers of the army. In his account of the battle of Tippecanoe, Mr. Walker uses the following language.

"General HARRISON received a shot through the rim of his hat. In the heat of the action his voice was frequently heard, and easily distinguished, giving his orders in the same calm, cool, and collected manner, with which we had been used to receive them in drill or parade. The confidence of the troops in the General was unlimited."

In the battle at Tippecanoe, Kentucky lost many of her bravest men, yet the legislature immediately passed the following resolution:—

"*Resolved*, That in the late campaign against the Indians on the Wabash, Governor W. H. Harrison has, in the opinion of this legislature, behaved like a hero, a patriot and a general; and that for his cool, deliberate, skilful, and gallant conduct in the late battle of Tippecanoe, he deserves the warmest thanks of the nation."

Complimentary resolutions were also passed by the legislature of Indiana, mentioning the "integrity," "superior capacity," and "important services" of the Governor. The militia who served in the campaign, immediately upon their return, held a meeting, at which they expressed unanimously their entire confidence in their commander; stating that their success was owing "to his masterly conduct in the direction and manœuvring of the troops."

The opinion of the government with respect to the action, is nobly given in a message from the excellent President Madison to Congress, under the date of December 18, 1811. The Executive conveyed his opinion in the following language:—

"While it is deeply to be lamented, that so many valuable lives have been lost in the action which took place on the 7th ult., Congress will see with satisfaction the dauntless spirit and fortitude victoriously displayed by every description of troops engaged, as well as the collected firmness which distinguished the commander, on an occasion requiring the utmost exertion of valor and discipline."

No one, with these facts before him, can question the courage of WILLIAM HENRY HARRISON. He was not one to be frightened by powder and ball, and the man who would attempt to tear one leaf from the glorious chaplet which encircles his brow, is no republican and deserves not the name of American. The soldiers of a republic *must be* patriots. They have no title of nobility to look forward to—they have no recompense but the applause of their countrymen, and the proud consciousness of having done their duty.

Immediately after the action, those opposed to the war claimed a part of the glory of the day for Colonel BOYD, which claim however was resisted by ail the army, and by none more strenuously than Colonel BOYD's corps itself. A drum-head court marshal was called to try the negro prisoner already mentioned, and Colonel BOYD was appointed president. The prisoner was convicted of deserting to the enemy, under circumstances from which it was concluded that he had returned to the camp for the purpose of assassinating the Governor. He was sentenced to suffer death. The sentence was approved, and he was to be executed in one hour, but the troops could not be called from their labor to witness his death.

We are not writing a defence of HARRISON. He requires nothing of the kind. We are giving a fair and unprejudiced account of his life from facts, and we leave the facts to speak for themselves. In a letter to Governor SCOTT of Kentucky, in speaking of the negro, MR. HARRISON thus writes:—

"The fact was that I began to pity him, and could not screw myself up to the point of giving the fatal order. If he had been out of my sight he would have been executed; but when he was first taken, General WELLS and Colonel OWEN, who were old Indian fighters, as we had no irons to put on him, had secured him after the Indian fashion. This is done by throwing a person on his back, splitting a log and cutting notches in it to receive the ankles, then replacing the severed parts, and compressing them together with forks, driven over the log into the ground. The arms are extended and tied to stakes secured in the same manner. The situation of a person thus placed, is as uneasy as can possibly be conceived. The poor wretch thus confined lay before my fire, his face receiving the rain that occasionally fell, and his eyes constantly turned upon me, as if imploring mercy. I could not withstand the appeal, and I determined to give him another chance for his life. I had all the commissioned officers assembled, and told them that his fate depended upon them. Some were for executing him, and I believe that a majority would have been against him, but for the interference of the gallant SNELLING. "Brave comrades," said he, "let us save him. The wretch deserves to die; but as our commander, whose life was more particularly his object, is willing to spare him, let us also forgive him. I hope, at least, that every officer of the 4th regiment will be on the side of mercy." SNELLING prevailed; and BEN was brought to this place, where he was discharged."

"During the time of the contest," says MCAFFEE, "the Prophet kept himself secure on an adjacent eminence, singing a war-song. He had told his followers that the Great Spirit would render the army of the Americans unsuccessful, and that their bullets would not hurt the Indians, who would have light, while their enemies would be involved in darkness. Soon after the battle commenced, he was informed that his men were falling. He told them to fight on, it would soon be as he predicted, and he began to sing louder."

At the time of the battle, TECUMTHE was still at the south, and when he returned was much exasperated, surprised, and mortified at the conduct of the Prophet. He saw at once that he must take a decided stand, and he did so, in favor of the English. The defeat of the Indians had in a measure, opened their eyes with respect to the power of the Prophet. The blow had been struck too soon. TECUMTHE was not yet ready. He had not enlisted all he wished. The opposing forces at the battle are stated by one authority to have been about equal—by another, it is said the Indians out numbered the Americans, by at least two hundred. The enemy never showed more courage. Thirty-eight warriors were left dead upon the field, and many more only lived to reach the town. The number of their wounded has never been, accurately ascertained.

The Americans had about fifty killed, and nearly one hundred wounded, out of eight hundred troops engaged.

TECUMTHE and his brother, were seen for the last time previous to their joining the British, at Fort Wayne. TECUMTHE then told the commander that he was going to Malden, "to receive from the British twelve horse-loads of ammunition for the use of his people at Tippecanoe." A letter from the commander said that the Prophet arrived there on the 12th of July, 1812, with one hundred Winnebagoes and Kickapoos and had completely duped the Indian agent with professions of friendship. While here a message came from TECUMTHE advising his brother to unite the Indians as soon as possible for a decisive blow upon Vincennes, and send the women and children beyond the Mississippi. The next day OL-LI-WA-CHI-CA sent a reply, and the messengers stole the commander's horses to carry them forward.

The whole of the day of the battle was occupied in fortifying the camp: burying the dead, and assisting the wounded. On the 8th, the town was reconnoitered. It was well fortified, but totally deserted. A large quantity of corn; all the household utensils and some guns and ammunition were found. Some dead bodies were discovered in the houses, and quite a number half buried in the gullies. On the 9th, the army prepared to return. Every wagon was required to transport the wounded. The Governor explained to the officers the necessity of destroying the baggage, and set the example by ordering all his own camp furniture to be broken and burned. At the block house on the Wabash the wounded were placed in boats, while the rest of the army continued their way to Vincennes, by land.

In December, several chiefs came to Vincennes to settle all difficulties, and in March, others came from all the tribes but the Shawanees.

CHAPTER XVIII.

Little Turtle writes to Governor Harrison—Arrival of Deputies—Council at Mississinniway—Another at Malden—Conduct of the British and Indians—the United States declare war against Great Britain—Dinner to Harrison—His letter to the Government—Governor Harrison appointed Major General by Brevet, by Governor Scott—Winchester appointed to the command, and Harrison appointed Brigadier General—Troops induced to march through General Harrison's advice.

ON the 25th of January, 1812, the LITTLE TURTLE, previously mentioned, wrote to Governor HARRISON, from Fort Wayne. This was in answer to a message sent to the Miami and Eel-River Indians. The TURTLE regretted the battle of Tippecanoe, yet thought it would "be the means of making the peace which ought to exist, respected." He stated that all the Prophet's followers, except two camps of his own tribe had left him. That TECUMTHE had just joined him with only eight men—that the Indians would visit Vincennes whenever requested by the Governor—and that he (the TURTLE) would inform the Governor of all the movements of the Indians.

Unfortunately the services of the TURTLE were cut short about six months after. He died at Fort Wayne, July 14, 1812, and was buried with the honors of war. His disease was reported "gout," by the army surgeon.

In February, eighty deputies, from all the tribes engaged in the late troubles, except the Shawanees, reached Fort Harrison, on their way to Vincennes. In consequence of a private notice of a design upon his person, the Governor sent a messenger to meet them, and demand the reason of their coming in so large a body. On their arrival they delivered up their arms, and evinced the subdued spirit of men taught to honor the genius and power of him with whom they came to treat.

Many of the protestations now made, were all deceptions, as we find most of the same men meeting a war council of the British, in May following, at Mississinniway, and directly after, again at Malden, at which last, ELLIOT, the

Indian agent, and the British commanding officer were present. At the first, the Wyandots began, censuring the Shawanees for their late conduct. TECUMTHE replied, and said that he too was very sorry for the affair on the Wabash, but that all difficulties with Governor HARRISON had been satisfactorily arranged. He also stated, that had he been at home, the battle would never have been fought. He then in turn, censured the Potawatamies. The latter replied, calling the Prophet and his followers, "vagabond," TECUMTHE was answering this, when he was stopped by the Delawares, who wished to proclaim peace throughout the land. The council was rather for peace. At the subsequent meeting at Malden, ELLIOT asked the Wyandots if they had not advised the tribes to remain neutral? To this, WALK-IN-THE-WATER made a spirited reply, throwing up to the English, their conduct at Fort Miami, in 1794, and concluding thus:—"We say again, we do not wish to have any thing to do with the war. Fight your own battles, but let us, your red children, enjoy peace."

The speaker was interrupted by ELLIOT, who told him he would hear no more "American talk." ROUND-HEAD then came forward and took hold of the wampum of ELLIOT. TECUMTHE and OL-LI-WA-CHI-CA followed, but the Wyandots left the council, and re-crossed the river to Brownstown. The Brownstown Wyandots were subsequently forced to ally themselves with the British.

June 18th, 1812, war was declared against Great Britain by the United States. The western governors entered with great spirit upon preparations of defence for their respective states. In expectation of a war, the English had inflamed the minds of the Indians, and their barbarities now became more frequent and more alarming. The settlers deserted their farms and fled to Vincennes with their families, to the protection of Governor HARRISON. The war was popular, and they all were ready to take the field, if required. In this excitement—when the rich and the poor, the learned and the unlearned, were flocking to the defence of their country; all with one voice, called for Governor HARRISON to lead them against their enemies, and to his hand confided their families, honor and property.

The Governor of Kentucky requested a conference, and MR. HARRISON repaired immediately to Frankfort. The former received his friend at the head of the militia, with the firing of cannon and the acclamations of the populace. All the citizens rushed forward to meet him, and to shake the hero by the hand.

He remained several days at Frankfort, wholly occupied with maturing plans for the defence of the country. While in Kentucky, a public dinner was given to him at Lexington, at which he delivered his opinion in an eloquent speech. The company was composed of ardent friends of the war, and he was urged to commit his sentiments to writing and address them to the Secretary of War. To this he objected, until assured by MR. CLAY, one of the persons present, that such a letter would be well received by the government. The following is an extract from the letter alluded to, which was writen, August 10th:—

"If it were certain that General HULL would be able, even with the reinforcement which is now about to be sent to him, to reduce Malden and retake Macinac, there would be no necessity of sending other troops in that direction. But I greatly fear that the capture of Macinac will give such eclat to the British and Indian arms, that the northern tribes will pour down in swarms upon Detroit, oblige General HULL to act entirely upon the defensive and meet, and perhaps overpower, the convoys and reinforcements which may be sent him. It appears to me, indeed, highly probable that the large detachment which is now destined for his relief, under Colonel WELLS, will have to fight its way. I rely greatly upon the valor of those troops, but it is possible that the event may be adverse to us, and if it is, *Detroit must fall*, and with it every hope of re-establishing our affairs in that quarter until the next year." * * * "There are other considerations which strongly recommend the adoption of this measure. I mean the situation of Chicago, which must be in danger, and if it is not well supplied with provisions, the danger must be imminent."

This letter was prophetic. Macinac had already fallen. Five days after Chicago was taken, and a few days after that, Detroit fell into the hands of the enemy. The surrender of HULL, left the whole frontier exposed.

Twelve hundred militia were embodied in Ohio, to march under Brigadier General TUPPER to the assistance of HULL. Kentucky had organized 5,500 men. Most of these were volunteers—young gentlemen of talent and fine prospects, farmers and mechanics of standing and character. Colonels ALLEN and HARDIN, eminent lawyers; Major MADISON state auditor; Colonels SCOTT and LEWIS experienced Indian fighters; Captain SIMPSON, formerly speaker of the House of Representatives of Kentucky; the Rev. SAMUEL SHANNON, who had served as a lieutenant during the revolution, and now went out as volunteer chaplain.

The troops were reviewed by Governor SCOTT on the 16th of August, and addressed by the Rev. JAMES BLYTHE, and HENRY CLAY. "At the very moment," says Judge HALL, "when the dastardly HULL was consummating an act of unparalleled meanness, by surrendering an important post, and a gallant army, without striking a blow for the honor of our flag—the unrivalled orator of Kentucky was pouring out those strains of fervid eloquence, which would have kindled up the latent spark of courage in bosoms less generous than those to which he appealed, and to which the sons of the hardy pioneers responded in bursts of patriotic enthusiasm."

The manner of, and reasons for General HARRISON's being selected to command these brave men, are clearly recorded by MCAFFEE, whose account we copy:—

"A few days before the actual attack on Detroit by General BROCK, an express had been sent by General HULL, to hasten the reinforcement which had been ordered to join him from Kentucky. By this conveyance, several of the principal officers of the army had written to their friends in Cincinnati, as well as to the Governor of Kentucky, stating their entire want of confidence in their commander, and their apprehensions of some fatal disaster from his miserable arrangements and apparent imbecility and cowardice. These letters, also, declared it to be the common wish of the army, that General HARRISON should accompany the expected reinforcements. He was also very popular in Kentucky, and was anxiously desired as their commander by the troops marching from that state to the north-western army. But the authority with which he had been invested by the President, did not entitle him to command any corps, which was not intended for operations in the western territories.

"The question of giving HARRISON the command of the detachment on the march from Kentucky for Detroit, presented great difficulties to the mind of Governor SCOTT. The motives to make the appointment were numerous. He had ample testimony of its being the wish of the army at Detroit. The fourth United States regiment[17] in particular, which had

---

[17] To this regiment belonged Mr. Adam Walker, from whose narration we have already made an extract, and must now take another. In speaking of General Harrison, Mr. Walker says. "He appeared not disposed to detain any man against his inclination, being endowed by nature with a heart as humane as brave; in his frequent addresses to the militia, his eloquence was formed to persuade, appeals were made to reason as well as feeling, and never were made in vain."

acquired so much fame at Tippecanoe, under the command of HARRISON, he was assured by an officer of that corps, were eager to see their old commander again placed over them. The same desire was felt by the Kentucky militia; and the citizens echoed their sentiments in every part of the state. To these may be added his own ardent attachment to Governor HARRISON, and entire confidence in his fitness for the command. The obstacles in the way of the appointment were, that HARRISON was not a citizen of Kentucky, the laws of which would not sanction the appointment of any other to an office in the militia; and that a Major General had already been appointed for the detached militia, one only being required and admissible in that corps. Had Governor Scott been capable of shrinking from his duty and the responsibility of the occasion, he might have easily evaded this delicate business, as the day on which he was deliberating upon it, was the last but one that he had to remain in office.

"That he might, however, neither act unadvisedly, nor appear to assume too much, in this situation, he determined to ask the advice of the governor elect, and such members of Congress, and officers of the general and state governments, as could be conveniently collected. At this *caucus*, composed of Governor SHELBY, the Hon. HENRY CLAY, speaker of the House of Representatives in Congress, the Hon. THOMAS TODD, judge of the Federal Court, &c., it was unanimously resolved to recommend to Governor SCOTT, to give HARRISON a brevet commission of Major General in the Kentucky militia, and authorize him to take command of the detachment now marching to Detroit; and to reinforce it with another regiment which he had called into service, and an additional body of mounted volunteer riflemen. The Governor conferred the appointment agreeably to their advice, which was received with general approbation by the people, and was hailed by the troops at Cincinnati with the most enthusiastic joy."

The object of the campaign being defeated by the contemptible conduct of HULL, General HARRISON commenced a system of discipline and organization, to which he devoted the most severe and personal attention. All the people looked to him with cheerful confidence, and the soldiers never thought of defeat under such a leader.

Shortly after General WINCHESTER was appointed by the War Department to the command, and HARRISON received a Brigadier General's commission, in the United States army. This appointment General HARRISON declined, until he could learn whether it would make him subordinate to General WINCHESTER. Again we copy from MCAFFEE:—"The troops had confidently expected that General HARRISON would be confirmed in the command; and by this time he had completely secured the confidence of every soldier in the army. He was affable and courteous in his manners, and indefatigable in his attention to every branch of business. His soldiers seemed to anticipate the wishes of their general: it was only necessary to be known that he wished something done, and all were anxious to risk their lives in its accomplishment. His men would have fought better and suffered more with him, than with any other general in America; and whatsoever might have been the merits of General WINCHESTER, it was certainly an unfortunate arrangement which transferred the command to him at this moment. It is absolutely necessary that militia soldiers should have great confidence in their general, if they are required to obey with promptness, or to fight with bravery. The men were at last reconciled to march under WINCHESTER, but with the confident belief that HARRISON would be reinstated in the command; and which accordingly was done, as soon as the War Department was informed of his appointment in the Kentucky troops, and his popularity in the western country."

It was through the exertions of HARRISON, that many were persuaded to march under WINCHESTER. Overlooking and forgiving the slight of the government toward himself, he looked only to the requirements of his country, and the exposed situation of the settlements; and went personally among the soldiers and induced them to march with WINCHESTER. It was ever thus with MR. HARRISON—having only the welfare of his country at heart, he relinquished most cheerfully all selfish ends, and devoted his services to his native land, wherever, whenever and however, she required his labors.

CHAPTER XIX.

State of the country—Harrison relieves Fort Wayne—Winchester takes the command—Harrison appointed to the command of the western army—His example at bivouac—Discontent in the camp—Harrison's address and the result of it—Object of the campaign—Plan of operations—Successful expedition under Campbell—Orders from Government—Harrison advises the building of a fleet.

The capture of Hull, left not a fort in our hands, upon the upper lakes, nor any regular force. A frontier of immense extent and hundreds of widely scattered settlements, were left in a great measure, entirely unprotected. The English agents were urging the savages to the most barbarous murders, and even the British commanding officer appeared to feast with delight upon the blood and torture of Americans. When General Harrison reached Piqua, he was almost without provisions and arms. He had written to the Secretary of War, that there was but one piece of artillery (an iron four pounder) in the whole country, and that, unless immediately supplied, he would be obliged to put muskets in the hands of the cavalry. "The troops which I have with me," he writes, "and those which are coming from Kentucky, are, perhaps, the best materials for forming an army that the world has produced." Yet he had no one upon whom he could call for assistance in training these noble fellows, except Captain Adams, and he was now sick.

Hearing that Fort Wayne was invested by the Indians, he pushed forward to that post. The enemy fled on his approach and he had the satisfaction of relieving an important fortress without loss of a man. He now sent out detachments to scour the country, and the Indian towns and corn fields were destroyed, in all the surrounding country. Thus the enemy was completely crippled, and could make no headway against the Americans.

Shortly after this, General Winchester arrived to take the command. He had served in the revolution, but was now advanced in years, and had lived a life of ease and elegant luxury, which unfitted him for the service. The troops were dissatisfied, and, as we have stated in the last chapter, were only reconciled through the exertions of General HARRISON himself.

The latter now left the army and was returning to his residence in Indiana, when he met an express conveying to him a letter from the Secretary of War, appointing him to the command of the north-western army. The letter, which will be found in our appendix, conferred upon General HARRISON the most extensive and important command, ever intrusted to any officer of the United States—WASHINGTON and GREENE only excepted. It concluded with these remarkable words—"You will command such means as may be practicable, exercise your *own* discretion, and act in *all* cases according to *your own* judgment." At the same time the Secretary also wrote to Governor SHELBY, that it had been determined to place the command in the hands of an officer, who possessed military character, a knowledge of the country and the confidence of the public. "General HARRISON has been appointed to the chief command," he continues, "with authority to employ officers, draw from the public stores, and every other practicable source, all the means of effectuating the objects of his command."

It is only necessary here to remark, that President MADISON, at the time he made this appointment, had known General HARRISON for about twelve years. As Secretary of State under JEFFERSON, MR. MADISON had access to the voluminous correspondence of General HARRISON, and it was with a perfect knowledge of his character that the command of the army was given.

General HARRISON now proceeded to St. Mary's and Defiance, where he found General WINCHESTER encamped. The march was forced, and the soldiers suffered exceedingly. No tents were in the army, and all shared alike the hardships of the season. A halt was not ordered until dark, and then all, except the guards, would wrap up in their blankets, and throw themselves down upon the bare ground. One evening they encamped on the banks of the Au Glaize, in a flat beech bottom, and the rain fell in torrents during the whole night. There were no axes in the army, and many sat without fire, upon their saddles—others leaned against trees, or crept beneath fallen logs. Being separated from the baggage, the troops had nothing to eat or drink, and some began to murmur. The General sat at a small fire, wrapped in his cloak, but drenched to the skin with the falling torrents. He was surrounded by his staff, and to set an example to the soldiers, he called upon one of his officers to sing an Irish comic song. Another officer sang another song, the chorus of which was:—

"Now's the time for mirth and glee
Sing and laugh and dance with me."

The contrast between the frivolity of these words, and the howling of the tempest and the darkness of the forest, had a powerful effect upon the army. The spirit thus shown at head quarters spread through all the troops, and frequently after, when wading knee-deep in the mud, some noble soul would sing out,

"Now's the time for mirth and glee,"

and the chorus would be instantly repeated by the whole line.[18]

An interesting incident which occurred on the arrival of General HARRISON at WINCHESTER's camp, is recorded by MR. BUTLER.[19] Overcome by the fatigues of his march, General HARRISON retired to snatch a little repose, and his arrival was only know to a few officers.

He was soon after awakened by Colonel ALLEN and Major HARDIN, who informed him that ALLEN's regiment, exhausted by hard fare, had determined to return home. The General refused to interfere at that moment, but said he would manage the affair in his own way, and the officers retired. He however, immediately sent one of his aids to direct General WINCHESTER to order the alarm to be beat the next morning instead of the reveille. This diverted the spirits of the discontented troops, and brought all the men to their arms. General WINCHESTER having formed them into a hollow square, General HARRISON appeared on parade, much to the surprise of the soldiers who knew nothing of his arrival. This was a joyful sight to the men, and he at once addressed them. He regretted that there were many discontented in one of the Kentucky regiment. Although this was mortifying to himself, on their account, it was happily of little importance to the Government. He had more troops than he well knew what to do with, and was expecting yet others. It was fortunate that he had discovered the dissatisfaction early in the campaign, as

---

[18] Dawson.
[19] Author of the History of Kentucky.

it otherwise might have been mischievous to the public interests and disgraceful to the parties concerned. "Now, so far as the government is interested, the discontented troops, who have come to the woods with the expectation of finding all the luxuries of home and peace, have full liberty to return. I will order facilities for their immediate accommodation; but I cannot refrain from expressing the mortification I anticipate from the reception they will meet from the old und the young, who greeted them on their march to the scene of war, as their gallant neighbors. What will be their feelings when they see those whom they hailed as their generous defenders, now returning without striking a blow, and before their term of plighted service has expired? If their fathers do not drive back their degenerate sons to the field of battle to recover their wounded honor, their mothers and sisters will hiss them from their presence. If however the discontented men are disposed to put up with all the taunts and disdain which await them wherever they may go, they are at liberty to go back."

The effect of this address was electric. SCOTT, the senior Kentucky Colonel, called upon "his boys," to attest their attachment to their country and their general, by giving him three cheers. The air resounded with a joyful peal. Colonel LEWIS now culled for and received a similar demonstration from his men. With a feeling which almost choked his utterance, the brave ALLEN now appealed to the disaffected regiment. They threw up their voices in a loud shout, and returned cheerfully to their duty. From that time no troops were more faithful, "until the fatal day when most of them gave their lives to their country, on the bloody field of Raisin."[20]

The objects of the present campaign were to retake Detroit, and to expel the British from the territory of the United States—to protect the extensive frontier and reduce Malden, in upper Canada. The militia were badly armed and clothed, and no regular system for furnishing supplies had been established. Every article for the army was to be conveyed two hundred miles at least, through the wilderness, in wagons or on pack-horses.

The ground was swampy and extremely difficult to be passed. All the various departments which should have been filled by proper officers, were left almost solely to HARRISON's personal supervision. The lakes presented

---

[20] Judge Hall.

innumerable inlets where the enemy could land, and which were almost indefensible from their very localities.

The General drew up his plan of operations at the outset. The Rapids of the Miami of the Lakes, was the point of concentration, from which the principal movement against the enemy was to be made. The military base extended from upper Sandusky on the right, to Fort Defiance on the left. The right division, a Virginia and a Pennsylvania brigade, he commanded in person. Three Kentucky regiments at Fort Defiance, were commanded by General WINCHESTER, who was directed to attend for the present, chiefly to forwarding supplies for the main expedition against Detroit. A brigade of Ohio militia formed the centre, at Fort M'Arthur, and was commanded by Brigadier General TUPPER. Each corps had a separate line of operations, terminating at the Rapids. General HARRISON passed along the line, employing himself in expediting the march of the troops, and forwarding artillery and supplies. Fort Winchester was completed; and Fort Barbee, at St. Mary's, and Fort Amand, or the Au Glaise, were erected, and a fortified work was thrown up at Colonel JENNING's encampments. Boats and canoes were also built.

Some operations in the field, for driving back the enemy took place in the fall. Two under General TUPPER, which were unsuccessful. Lieutenant Colonel CAMPBELL, was sent by General HARRISON, with six hundred men, to attack a fortified and well defended Indian village. The affair was gallantly conducted, and the town was taken after an action of one hour. The Colonel had 8 men killed, 48 wounded, and a large number rendered unfit for service, by fatigue, frost and sickness. In the general order, HARRISON applauded the perseverance, fortitude and bravery of Colonel CAMPBELL's troops. Hid orders to spare the women, children, and the prisoners, were punctually obeyed, for which he highly extolled the whole detachment. The order contained the following noble and beautiful sentiments:—

"Let an account of murdered innocence be opened in the records of heaven, against our enemies alone. The American soldier will follow the example of his government; and the sword of the one will not be raised against the fallen and helpless, nor the gold of the other be paid for the scalps of a massacred enemy."

As the season advanced, new difficulties presented themselves, and he was obliged to relinquish the idea of taking Malden during that campaign, as it could only be done at a great sacrifice of life and risk of failure. He so wrote to the government, stating that the project was not warrantable under any correct military principles. In reply, MR. MONROE then Secretary of War, said, that from the distance and imperfect knowledge of things on the frontier, it was impossible for the President to decide, to his own satisfaction or to the advantage of the public. "No person," continues MR. MONROE, "can be so competent to that decision as yourself, and the President has great confidence in the solidity of the opinion you may form. He wishes you to weigh maturely this important subject *and take that part which your judgment may dictate.*"

General HARRISON now advised the building of vessels to contend with the English upon the lakes. This advice was soon after followed, and the wisdom of the suggestion was evinced by repeated naval victories.

CHAPTER XX.

Attack on Fort Harrison—Massacre on the Pigeon Roost Fork—Volunteers from Kentucky—Expeditions of General Hopkins—Expedition of Governor Edwards and Colonel Russell—Orders of General Harrison—Winchester neglects to regard the instructions of General Harrison—Lewis advances to Frenchtown—Gallant action at Frenchtown—Massacre of the River Raisin—Conduct of the brave Madison—Conduct of the British government—Harrison's surprise at Winchester's conduct—Exertions of the former to reinforce the latter.

A body of Kickapoos and Winnebagoes attempted to gain admission to Fort Harrison, on the 3d of September. Captain ZACHARY TAYLOR, the commandant, kept the garrison on the alert. On the day following an assault was made, and the enemy gallantly repulsed. Foiled in this, the Indians fell upon the settlements on the Pigeon Roost Fork of White River, and cruelly tortured and murdered twenty one men, women and children. The savages were in the pay of the British government. An escort of provisions of 13 men, was surprised near Fort Harrison, and cut to pieces. In Illinois and Missouri the most outrageous cruelties were committed, and many of the settlements were completely deserted. The veteran Colonel RUSSELL, U. S. A., sent a band of volunteers from Fort Harrison to Illinois, and assisted the Governor of that Territory in organizing the militia.

The points to be defended were scattered over a vast region of country, and though the care of it fell upon General HARRISON, officers in the distant sections were frequently obliged to act for themselves, not having time to receive orders from head quarters. The patriotic Governor SHELBY appealed to the noble Kentuckians, and 2,000 mounted volunteers immediately assembled to defend the exposed border. The excess was so great, that many were necessarily rejected. One veteran belonging to a company not accepted, remarked, "Well, well, Kentucky has often glutted the market with hemp, flour and tobacco; and now she has done it with volunteers."[21]

---

[21] Judge Hall.

By General HARRISON's appointment, these troops were assembled at Vincennes, in the beginning of October, and General SAMUEL HOPKINS, of the Kentucky militia assumed the command. He marched against the Kickapoo villages, but being deceived by the guides, and in want of provisions, the expedition failed, and returned. A court of inquiry afterward relieved General HOPKINS from all censure, and the frontier was for some time after, in a state of apparent safety. General HOPKINS was despatched by General HARRISON in November, at the head of a body of infantry, against the Indians on the Wabash. On the 19th, the detachment reached the Prophet's town, which was destroyed. A Kickapoo and a Winnebago village met the same fate.

About the same time Governor EDWARDS, of Illinois, and Colonel RUSSELL surprised the principal village of the Kickapoos, at the head of Peoria Lake, killed a large number of warriors, destroyed their corn, and captured about 80 horses.

General HARRISON had directed General WINCHESTER to advance to the Rapids. The former arrived at upper Sandusky, December 18th, but no word had yet been received of the movement commanded. Another order was now sent to WINCHESTER—that as soon as he had procured 20 day's provisions, he was authorized to make the advance previously directed.

When at the Rapids, he was to commence building huts to induce the enemy to believe that he was going into winter quarters. He was also to construct sleds for the expedition against Malden, but to lead the men to suppose they were for transporting provisions from the interior. The different lines were to meet at the Rapids, and a choice detachment would be marched on rapidly to Malden.

Having heard subsequently, that TECUMTHE had collected a large force on the head waters of the Wabash, and apprehending that the advance of the left wing would afford the chief an opportunity to destroy the provisions left on the line, General HARRISON sent another despatch to General WINCHESTER, recommending him to abandon the advance, and fall back with the greater part of his force to Fort Jennings. In the meanwhile, however, WINCHESTER had commenced his march for the Rapids, and did not conceive that he was bound by the last instruction to alter his plan. He had sent forward MR. LESLIE COMBS, a brave young Kentuckian, to inform the commander-in-chief of his movement. Accompanied by a single guide, MR. COMBS performed the journey on foot.

On the 10th of January, WINCHESTER reached the Rapids and fortified a good position on the north bank of the river, and a few days after several messengers arrived from the river Raisin, with intelligence that a body of Indians was moving toward the settlement, and protection was requested. Early on the 17th Colonel LEWIS with 550 men, was sent to the Raisin, and later in the same day, Colonel ALLEN was despatched with 110 more. An express from Colonel LEWIS, at Presque Isle, brought word that 400 Indians were at the Raisin, and that Colonel ELLIOT was expected from Malden, with a detachment of British and Indians, to attack the camp at the Rapids. This intelligence was then forwarded to head quarters.

On the 16th of January, General HARRISON learned; from General PERKINS, who was stationed at lower Sandusky, that a battalion had been solicited from the latter by General WINCHESTER, who was meditating a movement against the enemy. General HARRISON became exceedingly alarmed at this information, so contrary to his views and directions, yet made every exertion to get forward artillery and provisions. The commander-in-chief knew well the imprudence of attempting any movement unless well prepared and with a complete plan organized.

Colonel LEWIS pressed forward and found the enemy prepared to meet him at Frenchtown. An attack was resolved upon. The companies of MCCRACKEN, BLEDSOE and MATSON, commanded by ALLEN, formed the right; those of HAMILTON, WILLIAMS and KELLY, under Major GRAVES, the left; those of HIGHTOWER, COLLIER and SABRES, under Major MADISON, the centre; and those of HICKMAN, GLAVES and JAMES, under Captain BALLARD, the advanced guard. The enemy, posted among the houses, were soon dislodged by GRAVES and MADISON. The retreating foe was met by ALLEN, and driven to the woods.

Here a desperate but short engagement took place, and the English were driven for two miles before the continual charge of the bold Kentuckians, though the latter had made a forced march that day, of eighteen miles over ice. In noticing the action, General HARRISON said, "the troops amply supported the double character of Americans and Kentuckians." Our loss, 12 killed, 55 wounded. The enemy had 100 regulars and 400 Indians in the field, under Major REYNOLDS, and their loss was much heavier than ours.

Instead of retiring after this brilliant affair, LEWIS determined to maintain his position. General WINCHESTER approved his decision,[22] and hastened forward to support the Colonel, with 250 men. These arrived at Frenchtown on the evening of the 20th. The troops under LEWIS were protected from musketry by the garden pickets in the town, while the reinforcement was without cover, in the open field. Though no movement was made by the enemy until the morning of the 22d, yet not even a picket guard had been stationed upon any of the roads. During the night of the 21st, the British had come up, unobserved, and at daylight fired bombs, balls, and grape shot, from heavy pieces of artillery, at a distance of only three hundred yards. The reinforcement was sadly injured by the fire of the enemy, and soon fled across the river in the utmost confusion. The Indians gained our flank and rear, and butchered our soldiers most shockingly. General WINCHESTER and some of the troops were taken prisoners, and marched to the British camp. LEWIS still maintained his position and frequently repulsed the enemy, until the Indians gained his flank, when a general and indiscriminate massacre ensued. LEWIS was made a prisoner, and having had his coat stripped off, was conducted to the enemy's camp. ALLEN being badly wounded, surrendered to an Indian. Another assailed him, whom ALLEN struck dead at his feet, and was in turn shot down by a third savage. GARRETT, with 15 or 20 men, surrendered, and all but himself were butchered on the spot. A party of 30 were surrounded, and half of them slain at once.

GRAVES and MADISON still maintained their position within the picketing, and with their troops, behaved most gallantly. The former being severely wounded, sat down, and as he wiped the blood from his wound, exclaimed, "Never mind me, my boys—fight on!" PROCTOR, with ail his British regulars and savage allies, could not subdue this brave band of Americans. They gave not an inch to the foe.

A flag was at last sent to MADISON, with an order from WINCHESTER, by his aid Major OVERTON, to surrender. PROCTOR accompanied the flag, and made the demand, but Major MADISON replied, that he would not surrender, unless the safety of his men could be guaranteed. PROCTOR demanded, "Sir,

---

[22] It is to be greatly regretted, that after so signal a triumph, this fine detachment had not retired, or that General Harrison had not been apprised of these movements in time to support them.—*Judge Hall*.

do you mean to dictate *to me?*" "No," returned the intrepid Major, "I intend to dictate for myself; and we prefer selling our lives as dearly as possible, rather than be massacred in cold blood."

The surrender was made on express conditions—that the officers should retain their side arms—the sick and wounded to be carefully removed—private properly to be respected, and the prisoners protected by a guard. PROCTOR disregarded all stipulations, and handed over the prisoners to the Indians, who butchered them in cold blood. Some of their bodies were thrown into the flames of the burning village, while others, shockingly mangled, were left exposed in the streets. These awful deeds were continued for several days.[23]

"For the massacre at the River Raisin, for which any other civilized government would have dismissed, and perhaps have gibbeted the commander, Colonel PROCTOR received the rank of Major General in the British army!"[24]

The enemies of General HARRISON censured him for the advance of the unfortunate detachment, though the Commander-in-chief had no hand whatever in the movement; neither did he know of it until after it had marched. It was contrary to his orders, and explicit instructions communicated by his aid to General WINCHESTER. Colonel WOOD, in alluding to the first intelligence of the advance, received at head quarters, says:—

"This news for a moment paralyzed the army, or at least the thinking part of it, for no one could imagine that it was possible for him (WINCHESTER) to be guilty of so hazardous a step. General HARRISON was astonished at the imprudence and inconsistency of such a measure, which, if carried into execution, could be viewed in no other light than as attended with certain and inevitable destruction to the left wing. Nor was it a difficult matter to foresee and predict the terrible consequences which were sure to mark the result of a scheme, no less rash in its conception, than hazardous in its execution." * * * "What human means, within the control of HARRISON, could prevent the anticipated disaster, and save that corps which was already looked upon as lost—as doomed to inevitable destruction? Certainly none. What would a

---

[23] Hall and McAffee.
[24] McAffee.

TURENNE or an EUGENE have done, under such a pressure of embarrassing circumstances, more than HARRISON did?"

Again we copy from MCAFFEE:—

"With respect to reinforcing the detachment, a recurrence to facts equally proves that HARRISON is not blameable, as he made every exertion in his power to support it. It was not until the night of the 16th that he received information indirectly through General PERKINS, that WINCHESTER had arrived at the Rapids. By the same express he was advised that WINCHESTER *meditated* some unknown movement against the enemy. Alarmed at this information, he immediately made every exertion which the situation of his affairs required. He was then at Upper Sandusky, his principal deposit of provisions and munitions of war, which is sixty miles from the Rapids by the way of Portage River, and seventy-six by the way of Lower Sandusky; and about thirty-eight more from the River Raisin. He immediately sent an express to the Rapids, for information; gave orders for a corps of 300 men to advance with the artillery, and escorts to proceed with provisions; and in the morning *he proceeded himself* to Lower Sandusky, at which place he arrived in the night following, a distance of forty miles, which he travelled in seven hours and a half, over roads requiring such exertion, that the horse of his aid, Major HAKILL, fell dead on their arrival at the fort. He found there, that General PERKINS had prepared to send a battalion to the Rapids, in conformity with a request from General WINCHESTER. That battalion was despatched next morning, the 18th, with a piece of artillery; but the roads were so bad, that it was unable, by its utmost exertions, to reach the River Raisin, a distance of seventy-five miles, before the fatal disaster.

"General HARRISON then determined to proceed to the Rapids himself, to learn personally from General WINCHESTER his situation and views. At four o'clock on the morning of the 19th, while he still remained at Lower Sandusky, he received the information, that Colonel Lewis had been sent with a detachment, to secure the provisions on the River Raisin, and to occupy, with the intention of holding, the village of Frenchtown. There was then but one regiment and a battalion at Lower Sandusky, and the regiment was immediately put in motion, with orders to make forced marches for the Rapids; and General HARRISON himself immediately proceeded to the same place. On his way he met an express with intelligence of the successful battle, which had been fought on the preceding day. The anxiety of General HARRISON to push forward, and either prevent or remedy any misfortune which might occur, as soon as he was apprised of the advance to the River Raisin, was manifested by the great personal exertions which he made in this instance. He started in a sleigh with General PERKINS, to overtake the battalion under COTGROVE, attended by a single servant. As the sleigh went very slow, from the roughness of the road, he took the horse of his servant, and pushed on alone. Night came upon him in the midst of the swamp, which was so imperfectly frozen that the horse sunk to his belly at every step. He had no resource but to dismount and lead his horse, jumping himself from one sod to another which was solid enough to support him. When almost exhausted, he met one of COTGROVE's men coming back to look for his bayonet, which he said he had left at a place where he stopped, and for which he would have a dollar stopped from his pay, unless he recovered it. The General told him he would not only pardon him for the loss, but supply him with another, if he would assist him to get his horse through the swamp. By his aid, the General was enabled to reach the camp of the battalion.

"Very early on the morning of the 20th he arrived at the Rapids, from which place General WINCHESTER had gone, on the preceding evening, with all his disposable force, to the River Raisin. Nothing more could now be done, but wait the arrival of the reinforcements from Lower Sandusky."

"Instead of censure being due to HARRISON, he merits praise for his prudent exertions, from the moment he was apprised of WINCHESTER's arrival at the Rapids."

CHAPTER XXI.

The army retires to the Portage—Advances to the Rapids—Camp Meigs—Perry ordered to the Frontier—Landing of the British and Indians—Siege commenced—Brilliant sortie under Colonel Miller—Gallant charge of the Kentuckians under Dudley—The siege raised by the British.

GENERAL HARRISON was at the Rapids when the news of the disaster at the River Raisin reached that place. The force of the enemy was supposed to be much larger than our own, and a council of war concluded upon abandoning the present position of the left wing as untenable. The army retired the next day to the Portage, 18 miles, where the general concluded to wait for a reinforcement under General LEFTWICH, and then return to the Rapids. The latter did not arrive until the 30th of January, and on the 31st, the army now numbering 1,700, marched to the foot of the Rapids, and a good position was selected on the opposite side of the river from that previously occupied. All the troops were ordered forward, except a few companies left on the Au Glaize and St. Mary's. The advance soon amounted to 2,000 men, but it was now ascertained that the different corps were so much reduced, that the whole effective force was only 4,000.

Finding it impossible to advance upon Malden this season, General HARRISON had his camp strongly fortified under the direction of Captain WOOD. A substantial picketing inclosed an area 2,500 yards in circumference—8 double timbered block houses, 4 large batteries, and store houses and magazines were constructed. This position was called Camp Meigs, after the brave and excellent Governor of Ohio.

Having seen the garrison as well provided as it could be under the circumstances, General HARRISON repaired to Cincinnati to make arrangements for opening the spring campaign with the utmost vigor. He urged more strongly than ever, the necessity of having a fleet to compete with the English on Lake Erie, and the bold and daring PERRY, was at length sent to the frontier to build, launch, arm, and man a number of vessels.

General HARRISON having heard that the enemy intended an expedition against Camp Meigs, hastened to the scene of the expected action, and reached the camp on the 12th of April. He had written to the Governor of Kentucky for reinforcements, and now expected General CLAY with 3,000 men. A few companies despatched in advance, arrived before the camp was invested. On the 28th, it was ascertained that the enemy was advancing in full force.

On parade the commander-in-chief addressed the soldiers—roused their military pride and love of country, and he was answered by repeated and deafening shouts of applause.

Camp Meigs was near the battle ground where WAYNE had so completely routed the Indians and English, in 1794, and General HARRISON alluded to that event in a happy and forcible manner.[25]

The British took up a position about two miles from Camp Meigs on the opposite shore, while the Indians landed on this side and surrounded the American camp. Both armies commenced necessary works. On the morning of the 1st of May, the English artillerists were at their guns. Orders were given in the American camp, for the tents to be struck. In a few minutes the canvas was removed, and nothing was to be seen but a long breast work of earth, behind which the army was securely encamped. The Americans had erected a grand traverse, 12 feet high, running entirely across the camp, upon a base 20 feet broad and 300 yards long. For five days the enemy threw a continuous shower of balls, but with very little effect. General HARRISON kept up a heavy fire in the meantime.

---

[25] General Harrison spoke thus. "Can the citizens of a free country, who have taken up arms to defend its rights, think of submitting to an army composed of mercenary soldiers, reluctant Canadians goaded to the field by the bayonet, and of wretched, naked savages? Can the breast of an American soldier, when he casts his eyes to the opposite shore, the scene of his country's triumphs over the same foe, be influenced by any other feelings than the hope of glory? Is not the army composed of the same materials with that which fought and conquered under the immortal Wayne? Yes, fellow soldiers, your general sees your countenances beam with the same fire that he witnessed on that occasion; and though it would be the height of presumption to compare himself to that hero, he boasts of being that hero's pupil. To your posts then, fellow citizens, and remember that the eyes of your country are upon you."

At midnight on the 4th, Captain OLIVER arrived at Camp Meigs, and informed General HARRISON that General CLAY would reach him at dawn the next morning with his glorious Kentuckians. HARRISON despatched Captain HAMILTON to CLAY with fresh orders, directing him to land 800 men, a mile and a half above Camp Meigs on the opposite side of the river, for an assault upon the British batteries. The rest of CLAY's troops were to land on this side and cut their way into the fort.

In landing, the boats were separated by the rapidity of the current, and it was some time before all could act together. Captain PETER DUDLEY, with 50 men, cut his way into camp without loss. The Indians annoyed the landing of Colonel BOSWELL, but he formed and returned their fire. HARRISON sent out Major ALEXANDER, with the Pittsburgh Blues and the Petersburgh volunteers, and the companies of NEARING and DUDLEY, to relieve BOSWELL. When joined by these troops, the Kentuckians had fought their way to the gates of the fort. They all now formed—charged the Indians, and drove them half a mile at the point of the bayonet. HARRISON now perceived from the battery on which he stood, a body of British and Indians, on the left and rear of BOSWELL, and recalled the troops. He now ordered a sortie against the enemy's batteries on this side.

The command was given to Colonel JOHN MILLER, of the regulars, and the detachment numbered 350 men. The batteries were charged; the English driven off and their guns spiked. The enemy was completely discomfited, and 41 soldiers were made prisoners. The beaten force numbered 200 British regulars, 150 Canadians, and 500 Indians. MILLER returned to the fort triumphant. This action lasted 45 minutes, and our loss was 180 killed and wounded.

While this was going on, DUDLEY had landed on the opposite side of the river—charged the enemy's batteries at full speed, and pulled down the British flag without loss of a man. General HARRISON made signals for DUDLEY and his men to retire, but they loitered about examining the works. CAMPBELL was sent to recall them, but the Indians gathered on their flank, and attacked Captain COMB's company. DUDLEY again charged the foe, and drove them two miles. The enemy now rallying, attacked Major SHELBY, who had remained at the batteries. Some of his men were made prisoners and others driven to the boats. The Major rallied the rest; drove back the foe, and hastened to assist DUDLEY. A retreat was undertaken, but so great was the disorder that most of DUDLEY's men were taken prisoners.[26]

The noble DUDLEY and many of his gallant companions were now deliberately tomahawked, nor did General PROCTOR attempt to stay the massacre. He even allowed the Indians to fire at random upon the disarmed crowd.[27] These barbarities were stopped at last, by TECUMTHE,[28] who has since been styled, by one of the prisoners, "nature nobleman."

PROCTOR sent to Camp Meigs to summon HARRISON to surrender. The General replied that the message was an affront which must not be repeated. The action occurred on the 5th, and on the 8th, PROCTOR acknowledged that he was beaten by raising the siege and making the best of his way off. During the whole of the action, General HARRISON had stood in an exposed situation on one of the batteries, noting every movement.[29]

Leaving General CLAY in command, General HARRISON now visited other posts to look after the security of all. Governor MEIGS had raised a stout column of volunteers, and was leading them in person to relieve the American army, when the news of the retreat of the English reached him, and he disbanded his troops.

---

[26] Thus ended in signal disaster, an affair planned with wisdom, commenced with the brightest hopes, conducted for a time with skill and gallantry, and blasted in its event by the imprudence of a generous band, who suffered their impulse to lead them, instead of obeying the orders of their General. Had the instructions given to Dudley been pursued, or an ordinary degree of military judgment exercised, the events of that day would have been among the brightest in the annals of our country, and Kentucky saved from the mournful office of lamenting the loss of some of her noblest sons—*Judge Hall.*

[27] Those who preferred to inflict a still more cruel and savage death, selected their victims, and lead them to the gateway, and there, *under the eye of General Proctor, and in the presence of the whole British army, tomahawked and scalped them.*—Colonel Wood.

[28] This horrid work of destruction continued until the arrival of Tecumthe from the batteries. No sooner did the savage warrior behold the massacre, than he exclaimed, "For shame! it is a disgrace to kill a defenceless prisoner;" and stopped the carnage. One of our historians remarks, "In this single act, Tecumthe displayed more humanity, magnanimity and civilization, than Proctor, with all his British associates in command, displayed through the whole war on the North-western frontier."—*Judge Hall.*

[29] Vide Appendix.

CHAPTER XXII.

Colonel Johnson's mounted regiment—Skirmishes—Second siege of Fort Meigs—Council with the Indians—Harrison repairs to the Fort—Colonel Johnson ordered to Illinois—Order rescinded—Siege of Fort Meigs raised—Attack on Fort Stephenson—Orders to Croghan—His gallant defence of the Fort—Publication by the officers—Croghan's card.

COLONEL RICHARD M. JOHNSON[30] had suggested the organization of two regiments of mounted militia, to traverse the whole frontier. The Secretary of War submitted the plan to General HARRISON, who thought these troops could only be advantageously employed in the summer and fall. On the 26th of February, 1813, Colonel JOHNSON was authorized to raise a mounted regiment to serve under General HARRISON. The brave Colonel lost not an hour in obeying the instructions he had received, and proceeded at once to St. Mary's, and thence to Fort Wayne, with 900 daring Kentuckians.[31] In the march several demonstrations were made against the Indian villages.

In April, Fort Madison on the Upper Mississippi, was attacked, and soon after Fort Mason, by the Indians. In both assaults they were nobly repulsed. On the frontiers of Missouri and Illinois, repeated cruelties were committed by the savages. In the meanwhile the British had collected about 2,500 Indian warriors, at Malden.

General CLAY having learned that Fort Meigs was to be again besieged by the enemy, sent for the mounted regiment. JOHNSON addressed his men in a

---

[30] At that time a member of Congress from Kentucky, and now, 1840, Vice President of the United States.

[31] Colonel Johnson's brother James was appointed lieutenant colonel. The majors were, Duval Payne and David Thompson. The captains, R. B. McAffee (the author of the history of the late war,) Richard Matson, Jacob Elliston, Benjamin Warfield, John Payne, Elijah Craig, Jacob Stucker, James Davidson, S. R. Combs, W. M. Price and James Coleman. Jeremiah Kirtby was adjutant; B. S. Chambers, quarter-master; S. Theobalds, Judge Advocate; L. Dickinson, Sargeant Major; James Sugget, chaplain. The Surgeons were Drs. Ewing, Coburn and Richardson.

style of enthusiastic ardor, and marched immediately to Fort Meigs, where he arrived without meeting any opposition. General HARRISON was at Franklinton, when he received the news. He held a council with the chiefs of some of the friendly tribes, and told them they must now decide for or against the Americans. They all chose to be with us, and were informed that he would send them word when their services were required. "But you must conform to our mode of warfare," said he, "and you are not to kill defenceless prisoners, old men, women, or children."[32]

The commander-in-chief left Franklinton immediately for Fort Meigs, where he arrived by forced marches on the 28th of June, with 800 men of the 24th regiment of U. S. infantry, under Colonel ANDERSON. At the pressing solicitation of Governor EDWARDS of Illinois, General HARRISON received a communication from the War Department, instructing him to order Colonel JOHNSON to repair to Kaskaskia with his mounted regiment, and report to General HOWARD, then commanding in Missouri. This order created great indignation among the mounted men, and the patriotic Colonel at once wrote to General HARRISON, stating that his men were at Lower Sandusky, and desired to remain under the command of a general in whom they all had confidence. He stated also, that the horses were much jaded, and required rest. That his men were anxious for employment, and that he and they would cheerfully obey any orders coming from General HARRISON "at every hazard." Upon the receipt of this letter, which will be found in our appendix, General HARRISON addressed the War department, and the order for detaching the regiment to Illinois was rescinded.

The Indians again filled the country in the vicinity of Fort Meigs, early in July. TECUMTHE and DICKSON, an active partizan among the British Indians, had under their command 5,000 warriors.

---

[32] "He remarked, that by *their* conduct he would be able to determine whether the British could restrain the Indians employed by them; for if the Indians fighting with him, should abstain from such atrocities, the British would have equal influence with their own allies. He humorously told them that General Proctor had promised to deliver *him* into the hands of Tecumthe, to be treated as that warrior might determine. 'Now if I can succeed in taking Proctor,' said he, 'You shall have him for your prisoner, *provided* that you will agree to treat him as *a squaw*, and do him no other harm than to dress him in petticoats; for he must be a coward who would kill a defenceless prisoner.'"—*Hall's Memoir.*

Leaving Fort Stephenson,[33] under the command of Major CROGHAN, with 160 regulars, General HARRISON established his head quarters at Seneca Town, nine miles further up the river, and began to fortify his camp. At this time he had but 140 regulars with him, but 450 more arrived soon after. From Seneca Town he could fall back upon Upper Sandusky, or proceed to Fort Meigs by a secret route; The two latter were points to be defended.

On the 28th of July, the siege of Fort Meigs was abandoned, and the enemy prepared for a grand attack upon Sandusky. Fort Stephenson was surrounded by commanding heights, and the orders to Major CROGHAN were—"Should the British approach you in force, with cannon, and you can discover them in time to effect a retreat, you will do so immediately." "You must be aware, that the attempt to retreat in the face of an Indian force would be vain. Against such an enemy your garrison would be safe, however great the number."[34]

Anticipating an attack on Fort Stephenson or his head quarters, directly after the siege of Fort Meigs was raised, General HARRISON called a council of war, which agreed with him in regard to Fort Stephenson, and all concluded that the garrison should be withdrawn. An order was, therefore, immediately sent to CROGHAN to "abandon the fort, set fire to it, and repair to head quarters." The messenger missed the way, and the order was not received until the next day, when, finding that the Indians were about the fort in large numbers, he sent an answer that he was determined to maintain the place. He wrote in this manner lest the note should fall, as he expected it would, into the hands of the enemy. The reason was not however known, and he was ordered to head quarters for disobedience of orders. When he came and explained the meaning, he was immediately reinstated in his command and returned to the fort.

During all these proceedings several little skirmishes took place, and a squadron of dragoons sent to Fort Stephenson with the order for CROGHAN's appearance at head quarters, found a party of Indians lurking near the fort, whom they pursued and cut down.

---

[33] Fort Stephenson was not a regular fortification. It had been a trading post, and consisted of a large house surrounded by pickets. General Harrison had enlarged it on one side, for a temporary depot for provisions, and had drawn a ditch round the whole, so as to render it safe from an attack by Indians. It was a mere outpost of but little importance. It was only calculated for a garrison of 200 men, and could not be defended against heavy artillery.

[34] Dawson. McAffee.

On the morning of the 31st of July, the enemy approached Fort Stephenson by water, and landed troops, with a light howitzer. CROGHAN was summoned to surrender, and told he could not be protected against the savages, should he be captured. The gallant young Major replied, "That when the fort should be taken, there would be none left to massacre; as it would not be given up while a man was able to fight." The fort was surrounded by 500 British regulars and 800 Indians, commanded by General PROCTOR. TECUMTHE, with 2,000 warriors, watched the road to Fort Meigs, to intercept reinforcements. A fire was opened by the enemy from the howitzer and some six pounders in the boats. CROGHAN had but one gun, a six pounder, which he moved and fired from place to place, to induce the foe to imagine that he had more artillery.

But little damage was done that day. On the day following the firing was continued, and in the evening the whole force of the enemy made a grand assault in two columns. One column was completely cut up by the six pounder, discharged from a musket embrasure. The other was as suddenly discomfited, by the incessant discharge of musketry kept up by Captain HUNTER. It was quite dark when the fighting ceased.

The English left a colonel, a lieutenant, and 25 privates dead in the ditch, and 26 were taken prisoners, badly wounded. Our loss was *one* killed, and only *seven* slightly wounded. The total loss of the enemy is supposed to have been 150 killed and wounded.

The British wounded which were left in the ditch *by their friends*, were relieved by Major CROGHAN, who passed water to them over the picketing, and opened a way through which such as chose crept into the fort, where every thing was done to relieve them.

Early the following morning, the English and Indians retreated in the utmost disorder.[35] The officers under CROGHAN in this gallant action, were Captain HUNTER, Ensigns SHIPP and DUNCAN, Lieutenants JOHNSON and BAYLOR of the 17th, ANTHONY and ANDERSON of the 24th, and MEEKS of the 7th.

---

[35] It will not be among the least of General Proctor's mortifications, to find that he has been baffled by a youth who has just passed his twenty-first year.—*General Harrison's Official Report.*

As soon as the intelligence of the splendid triumph of young CROGHAN was made known, HARRISON was most violently assailed and denounced by the opposers of MADISON's administration. When the newspapers containing this abuse reached the camp, the officers and privates were indignant at the outrage upon their commander. Those highest in rank immediately drew up a paper,[36] which was sent to the interior and published, in which they assert, that General HARRISON's measures were "dictated by military wisdom, and by a due regard to our own circumstances and to the situation of the enemy."

The gallant CROGHAN, not content with having signed the paper with the others, and disdaining to receive any credit at the expense of a general he loved for his wisdom and valor, published a card under his own name,[37] which at once silenced all the clamor among those who thought for themselves upon the subject. In this card he used these words:—"The measures recently adopted by him, (General HARRISON,) so far from deserving censure, are the clearest proofs of his keen penetration and able generalship."

When the reasons could be explained, it was found to be as CROGHAN had stated, and fresh proof was added to volumes already given, of the courage, care, and penetration of General HARRISON. While these operations were going forward, the General had kept the main point constantly in view, and devoted every spare moment to preparations for the invasion of Canada. Commodore PERRY had been directed to co-operate with him. The mounted regiment of Colonel JOHNSON, which had returned home, was recalled to the frontier. Governor MEIGS exerted himself to bring the sturdy Ohians forward, and Governor SHELBY, of Kentucky, resolved to lead himself a fresh band from his own state. This was done at the invitation of General HARRISON, who now found himself ready to make a demonstration upon the territory of the enemy.

---

[36] This paper will be found in our Appendix. It is dated, "Lower Seneca Town, Aug. 19, 1813," not three weeks after the action.

[37] See Appendix.

CHAPTER XXIII.

The armament of the fleets—Manning of the American vessels—Perry's orders—Order of battle—Position of the Niagara—Perry's courage—Surrender of the English fleet.

PERRY had built at Erie, from the stump, six vessels, and repaired four others. Those built were, the Lawrence, of 20 guns, two long 12s, and eighteen 24 pound carronades; the Niagara, of the same armament; the schooner Ariel, 4 guns, 18s and 24s; the schooner Scorpion, 2 guns, 32s; the schooners Porcupine and Tigress, each one 32. Those repaired, the Caledonia, 3 guns 24s and 32s; the Somers, two 32s; the Trippe and Ohio, one 32 each.

The British had six vessels at Malden, the sloop Little Belt, 3; the ship Detroit, 19; the brig Hunter, 10; ship Queen Charlotte, 17; schooner Lady Provost, 15 guns; and the Chippewa, 1 gun and 2 swivels.

The British vessels were all stout built, of solid oak, but ours were hastily put together, and only intended to carry guns and men. The Lawrence, Niagara, Caledonia, Ariel, and Scorpion, were good sailers—the rest were dull. Early in August, the heavier vessels were taken over the bar at the mouth of the river on the backs of camels, and in full sight of the enemy's fleet which lay off the harbor, and witnessed the whole operation. "These camels were long, broad, deep boxes, made of planks like scows, and perfectly water-tight, with holes in them to fill and sink, and pumps to exhaust them of water, and raise them so as to float with their upper edge high above the surface. These, placed on each side, and connected by strong beams, on which the vessels being placed when they were sunk; thus raised the vessels above the bar, when the camels were pumped out, and raised again by their own buoyancy."[38]

When Commander PERRY left Newport, he took with him 149 men and 3 boys, all of whom were volunteers. Many of these remained at Sackett's

---

[38] "Battle of Lake Erie, by the Hon. Tristam Burges." The whole account of Perry's victory is compiled from *Mr. Burges'* work.

Harbor, to serve under Commodore CHAUNCEY. The guns of the fleet had been mounted in the batteries on shore. The militia under General MEAD, then encamped in the neighborhood, united with the seamen, and a great number from HARRISON's army volunteered for the ships.

General HARRISON now saw the plan he had so long urged, in full success. The American fleet was upon the waters of Lake Erie, and under a commander in whom he had every confidence. At the earnest solicitation of PERRY, 100 men, under command of Captain ELLIOT, were sent from Ontario by Commodore Chauncey. These men had all been in service on the Lakes, and they went now on board the Niagara, the command of which was given to ELLIOT.

On the evening of the 9th of September, a council of war was held, at which the command was, "Engage each your designated adversary, in close action, *at half cable's length;*" and PERRY then told his officers that he could not better advise them than in the words of Lord NELSON—"If you lay your enemy alongside, you cannot be out of your place."

This day had been appointed by the President, at the request of Congress, a day of fasting, humiliation and prayer, and it was strictly observed by all in the army and navy.

In the order of battle the Lawrence, Commodore PERRY's flag ships, of 20 guns, was opposed to the Detroit, 19 guns; the Caledonia, Lieutenant HUNTER, 3 guns, to the Hunter with 10 guns; and the Niagara, Captain ELLIOT, 20 guns to the Queen Charlotte with 17 guns. The remaining American vessels were commanded by lieutenants, sailing masters and midshipmen.[39] In the British fleet there were one commodore and three captains. At daylight on the 10th the enemy was discovered, and the signal was given to get under weigh. For some time the enemy had the wind, but it soon changed so that our fleet were at windward. The British drew up in line. The orders of the preceding night were passed from ship to ship. PERRY hoisted his fighting flag with the words "Don't give up the ship," upon it, on the Lawrence. At the sight of it, all the crews gave three hearty cheers. PERRY brought the Lawrence close down upon the Detroit and went bravely to work. Lieutenant HUNTER, brought up the Caledonia according to orders.

---

[39] The Ohio was not in the action, having been previously sent down the Lake on other service.

"The Niagara," says Mr. BURGES, "was astern of the Lawrence, and the Caledonia abeam of the Queen Charlotte in the line of approach, when the action commenced. She, at first, discharged her first division; but when their shot fell short of the Queen Charlotte, Captain ELLIOT did not order the helm put up, and run down to within half cable's length of his adversary, the Queen Charlotte, but directed his lieutenant to *cease firing* with the carronades, and *fire* with his *long twelves only*. The Queen Charlotte had 20's to the Niagara's 24 pound carronades, but no long guns; and therefore, as she could neither reach the Niagara with her carronades, nor run up against the wind, and lay her alongside, she packed all sail, and run down to the aid of the Detroit and laid the Lawrence and the Caledonia alongside at half past 12 o'clock, M." * * * "The Lawrence for two and a half hours sustained the fire of the Detroit, and for two hours, that of the Detroit, Queen Charlotte, and most of that of the Hunter; forty-four guns, with all the marines, at half musket shot." The dead lay where they fell, until the action was over. Not a murmur was heard upon the deck of the Lawrence. PERRY was as cool as if on ordinary duty. "Why does not the Niagara come down and help us!" escaped from the wounded and dying. PERRY worked with his own hands at the last gun, and when that was disabled, he had only his little brother, 14 men and himself, alive and unhurt on board the Lawrence. Finding the Niagara did not come down, he exclaimed, "Lower the boat, and I will go and bring her down."

Taking his fighting flag under his arm, he left the vessel under the command of Lieutenant YARNALL, saying, as the boat pushed off—"I leave it to your discretion to strike or not; but the American colors must not be pulled down over my head to-day." PERRY left the Lawrence at half past two, and at a quarter before three, he hoisted his fighting flag on board the Niagara, which vessel was uninjured and had not lost a man. ELLIOT was, at his own request, sent to bring up the gun-boats which were astern. The Lawrence struck and dropped astern, and Lieutenant TURNER now brought up the Caledonia to fight the Detroit, taking the position abandoned by the Lawrence. PERRY was no sooner on the Niagara, than he *did* bring her down. "He broke through the enemy's line; passed between the Hunter and Detroit, at half pistol shot, thirty feet, from each; and from all his guns double shotted with round, grape canister, poured his broadsides into these devoted vessels. Rounding to, opposed to the taffrail of the Queen Charlotte, then, by her bowsprit, entangled in the mizzen rigging of the Detroit, he began a raking fire, from end to end of both their decks."[40] This ended the fight—the British vessels he had contended with struck at 10 minutes before 3—the rest a few minutes after. The loss in the American fleet;—in the Lawrence, 22 killed, 61 wounded; Niagara, 2 killed, 25 wounded; Caledonia, 3 wounded; Somers, 2 do.; Ariel, 1 killed, three wounded; Trippe, 2 wounded, and in the Scorpion, 2 killed.[41] The British lost 41 killed, and 94 wounded.

The killed were buried side by side at Erie, lamented by the tears of friends and foes, and the music and cannon of both fleets. The British commodore in his account says, "Captain PERRY has behaved in the most humane and attentive manner, not only to myself and officers, but to all the wounded."

PERRY wrote to General HARRISON:—"We have met the enemy, and they are ours." To the Secretary of the Navy, "It has pleased the Almighty to give to the arms of the United States a signal victory over their enemies on this lake. The British squadron consisting of two ships, two brigs, one schooner and one sloop, have this moment surrendered to the force under my command, after a sharp conflict."

---

[40] Tristam Burges.
[41] Letter of Dr. Usher Parsons, who was surgeon's mate in the American fleet, and had charge of *all* the wounded, to Dr. C. G. Perry, son of Commodore Perry.

CHAPTER XXIV.

Embarcation of the troops—Order of Battle—Battle of the Thames—Gallant charge of Colonel Johnson—Military skill of General Harrison—Death of Tecumthe—Capture of the British army—End of the war in Upper Canada.

COLONEL JOHNSON was again upon the frontier with his mounted Kentuckians. General MCARTHUR was at Fort Meigs, reducing the area of the works and making preparations to ship the heavy artillery and a part of the stores. Thirty wagons and a number of pack-horses arrived by the 1st of September, which were used for the transportations. Governor SHELBY soon arrived with a strong body of men, who were divided into eleven regiments. His aids were, General ADAIR and JOHN J. CRITTENDEN. Esquire.

General HARRISON was now determined to push the war into the enemy's territory. The artillery, stores and provisions were embarked on the 16th. The term of service for the Kentuckians under General CLAY having expired, they solicited and obtained permission to remain and accompany the expedition. They now proceeded with the stores. On the 20th, General HARRISON embarked with the regular troops under CASS and MCARTHUR. Between that and the 24th the remainder of the army followed to the place of rendezvous, at Put-in-Bay. HARRISON sailed with PERRY, to reconnoitre Malden, in the Ariel, on the 26th. Immediately on his return he issued a minute order of debarkation, march and battle. The next day the army landed, the commander-in-chief having first issued among the troops the following address:

"HEAD QUARTERS, ON BOARD THE ARIEL,
 "*September* 27, 1813.

"GENERAL ORDER.[42]—The General entreats his brave troops to remember that they are sons of sires whose fame is immortal. That they are to fight for

---

[42] This order was published in Niles' Register, of October 30, 1813, with the following heading.

the rights of their insulted country, whilst their opponents combat for the unjust pretensions of a master. *Kentuckians!*—remember the River Raisin! but remember it only whilst the victory is suspended. The revenge of a soldier cannot be gratified upon a fallen enemy."

The army landed,[43] but PERRY's victory and the advance of General HARRISON had cooled General PROCTOR so much, that burning the fort and navy-yard, he fled. The army encamped on the ruins of Malden, and HARRISON wrote to the War Department, that he should pursue the enemy the following day, though he had, he said, little hope of "overtaking him, as he has 1000 horses, and we have not one in the army." The inhabitants hid their property and fled, supposing that a banditti had come among them. Governor SHELBY issued an order to the Kentucky volunteers, requiring the inhabitants to be treated with justice and humanity, and that property should not be wantonly injured. HARRISON called his general officers together on the first of October and told them he had determined to pursue the enemy.[44]

October 5th, the enemy was overtaken. PROCTOR had chosen an excellent position—his left flanked by the river Thames, and his right by a swamp. Still further to the right, TECUMTHE was posted with his Indians. The American army was drawn up; the flanks and rear most strongly secured against the Indians. At this moment Colonel WOOD reported to the commander-in-chief

---

"*Glorious Harrison.*—The following general order, issued on the day of the debarkation of our troops in Canada, is one of the "unkindest cuts" the "bulwark of our religion," (England. So called by those who oppose the war) ever received, if there remains one particle of shame in her system."

[43] Commodore Perry landed with Harrison, and acted as his volunteer aid at the battle of the Thames.

[44] He informed them that there were but two ways of doing it—one of which was, to follow him up the strait by land—the other to embark and sail down Lake Erie to Long Point, then march hastily across by land twelve miles to the road, and intercept him. "But the Governor thinks, and so do I, that the best way will be to pursue the enemy up the strait, by land." The general officers unanimously concurred in the same opinion, together with General Adair, first aid to the Governor, who had been invited to the council. I have been thus particular in stating the facts relative to the determination to pursue the enemy, because it has been reported and believed that General Harrison never would have pursued farther than Sandwich, had it not been for Governor Shelby.—*McAffee.*

The fact is, there never was any difference of opinion between them, either as to the propriety of the pursuit, or the manner of performing it.—*Judge Hall.*

that the regular infantry of the enemy, was formed in open order. Judge HALL thinks that PROCTOR had heard that this mode of formation was practised by us in fighting the Indians, and that he had misapplied the principle. Be that as it may, PROCTOR had committed a woeful error, which the wisdom and military experience of General HARRISON at once told him he could turn to our advantage. Troops in open order, that is, with intervals of three or four feet between the files, can never resist a charge of cavalry. HARRISON instantly ordered Colonel JOHNSON to dash through the enemy's line with his mounted men, in column.

The command was brilliantly executed. The mounted men charged impetuously through the enemy's ranks—formed in their rear and attacked their broken line. The British threw down their arms, and an almost bloodless victory was obtained by the ease with which General HARRISON manœuvred his army, and the rapidity with which he took advantage of the errors of the enemy. The Indians behaved much better—they rushed upon the mounted men in the fiercest desperation. TECUMTHE pressed eagerly into the heart of the contest, encouraging his warriors with his voice, and throwing his tomahawk in deadly fury. Suddenly the cry of command which had urged them on, was hushed. The haughty chief had fallen.[45] His men now fled, leaving thirty three dead on the field, most of whom were found near TECUMTHE. He was killed in that part of the line, where Colonel JOHNSON was wounded, and by some it is supposed that he fell by the hand of the Colonel himself.

Thus ended the battle. The whole army of the enemy was captured, except a few that galloped off with General PROCTOR. He had promised to deliver

---

[45] The grave in which Tecumseh's remains were deposited by the Indians after the return of the American army, is still visible near the borders of a willow marsh, on the north line of the battle-ground, with a large fallen oak-tree lying beside. The willow and wild rose are thick around it, but the mound itself is cleared of shrubbery, and is said to owe its good condition to the occasional visits of his countrymen.—*Western Paper.*

Thus repose, in solitude and silence, the ashes of the *Indian Bonaparte.* In truth have they

―――― "Left him alone in his glory."
Thatcher's Indian Biography.

The British government granted a pension to his widow and family. The Prophet was supplied in like manner until his death, which took place a few years since.

HARRISON and his men *when taken*, to the tomahawk and scalping knife. He now trembled for the fate of his own worthless person should he fall into the hands of the Americans.

The loss of the British was 18 killed and 26 wounded. Prisoners taken, 600. Our loss was about the same in killed and wounded. Our army numbered less than 2,500, nearly all of whom were militia. The enemy had 845 regulars and 2,000 Indians in the field.

This brilliant victory[46] following so close upon Perry's glorious battle, closed the war in that quarter, and rescued the whole north-western frontier from the barbarities of the savages. There was a general rejoicing throughout the country, and even the enemies of HARRISON now openly acknowledged that he was a truly great man.

---

[46] The victory of Harrison was such as would have secured to a Roman General, in the best days of the republic, the honors of a triumph. He put an end to the war in the uppermost Canada.—*The Honorable Langdon Cheves.*

CHAPTER XXV.

Kentucky Volunteers disbanded—Harrison goes to Sackett's Harbor—Public rejoicings—Opinion of Simon Snyder—Democratic meeting at Harrowgate—Harrison's resignation—Perry's opinion of Harrison—Same by General McArthur.

ALL the artillery and military stores of the British army fell into the hands of the American troops. Among the former were three beautiful brass field pieces, which had been taken during the revolutionary war, and which were recovered by the English at the dastardly surrender of General HULL. During the pursuit of PROCTOR all HARRISON's baggage was carried in a valise, and his bed was a single blanket fastened over his saddle. This last he gave to Colonel EVANS, a wounded British officer. On the night after the battle of the Thames, he invited thirty-five British officers (prisoners of war,) to sup with, and all he had to place before them was fresh roast beef, without either bread or salt. This was the fare of the army, and he would never have better food than his soldiers.

On the return of the troops, the Kentucky volunteers were dismissed at Detroit, and the British Indians sent to General HARRISON, to ask for peace. An armistice was granted, that the general government might have time to consider the terms.

On the 22d of October, General HARRISON and suite, and Commodore PERRY, arrived at Erie, in the Ariel, from Detroit. They were received by the inhabitants with rapture—with the thunder of cannon, illuminations, and every demonstration of joy as the deliverers of the frontier. PERRY went to Newport, Rhode Island. General HARRISON, with about 1,500 troops went on the next day, and reached Black Rock on the 24th. Commodore BARCLAY, the commander of the late English fleet, accompanied HARRISON and PERRY.[47] On HARRISON's arrival at Fort Niagara, preparations were making

---

[47] Nile's Register, Vol. V.

for an expedition against Burlington Heights. These were arrested by an order from the Secretary of War, who was then upon the frontier, for HARRISON to bring his troops to Sackett's Harbor. At the latter place he left his men and proceeded forthwith to Washington, by the way of New York and Philadelphia. The account of the victory of the Thames had preceded the hero, and he was met with public rejoicings and hearty congratulations in every town on his route. From Niles's Register of November, 1813, we make the following extract:—

"HARRISON's Victory.—There was a general illumination in Philadelphia on the evening of the 27th ult., by recommendation of the major, such expressions of joy being prohibited by law, without his permission. Many of the public buildings in New York were illuminated in great style. The bells were rung and salutes from all the forts, from the navy yard and the flotilla. Such demonstrations of joy have been exhibited in almost every town and village we have heard from."

Again, in the same volume, NILES says:—

"Harrison's victory has been celebrated in Washington, Alexandria, Wilmington, (Del.) Philadelphia, and New York, by brilliant illuminations. In the latter, by *recommendation of the constituted authorities.*"

"From St. Louis, we have satisfactory accounts of the measures that have been taken to meet and punish the Indians in that quarter. But it is probable that HARRISON's victory has given peace to all the western country. The news of it will fly like wild fire among the savage tribes, and point out the *necessity of submission.*"

The author perfectly remembers the illumination in Philadelphia. The people were then all hurrahing for the Hero of the Thames, (though he had not yet reached that city,) except a few tories who were opposed to the war and would have cheerfully given back the whole country to the yoke of Great Britain. A crowd paraded the streets on the night of the celebration, and the windows of almost every tenanted house were brilliantly lighted. Bands of music, accompanied the immense concourse, and appropriate national airs were performed. The houses of a few well known tories were visited by the patriotic assemblage, and three awful groans given before the door of each, while the musicians played the Dead March to some, and the Rogue's March to others.

The excellent SIMON SNYDER, then governor of Pennsylvania, in his message to the Legislature at the following session, (December 10th, 1813,) used the following language:—

"The blessings of thousands of women and children, rescued from the scalping knife of the ruthless savage of the wilderness, and from the still more savage PROCTOR, rest on HARRISON and his gallant army."[48]

These are but a few of the notices of the victory. The papers of the day were filled with compliments to the hero, and we might occupy a much larger book than this, before we could give one half of the applause generously heaped upon his head at the time, and for years after. Before this, it was well known that HARRISON would never abandon a battle until victory crowned his efforts. When it was understood that he was about to invade Canada, the whole country rang with the tidings, and all felt convinced that he would conquer. There expectations were fully realized.

Among the proceedings of a celebration of the Fourth of July, in 1813, held at Harrowgate near Frankford, Philadelphia county, (Penn.) by the "Democratic Young Men," the following regular toast will be found. The President of the dinner was the staunch old democrat JONATHAN B. SMITH, Esq.: and DR. JOEL B. SUTHERLAND was the Secretary. The DR. likewise delivered the oration in the morning at the Universalist Church in Lombard street. It will be borne in mind that this toast was drank before General HARRISON gained the victory of the Thames:—

"GENERAL WILLIAM HENRY HARRISON—the WASHINGTON of the West—we look forward to his speedily avenging the barbarities of Tecumthe and his inhuman allies the British," 1 gun 9 cheers.[49]

The reader has already seen how soon this prophetic sentiment was realized. The toast had scarcely travelled to the frontier, when HARRISON had taken the whole British army, and the hostile Indians were bending at his feet, suing for peace.

When General HARRISON reached Washington, he was urged by the President to hasten to Cincinnati, to superintend measures then in anticipation. At this time, General JOHN ARMSTRONG was Secretary of War.

---

[48] Pennsylvania Legislative Documents.

[49] The whole proceedings may be found in the Weekly Aurora published in Philadelphia, in 1813.

He was notorious for his attempts to stir up a mutiny in the army of the revolution, in 1783, when it was about to be disbanded. From some prejudice conceived against him, in the plan of the campaign of 1814, submitted to the President by the Secretary, General HARRISON was confined to the command of the 8th military district, which included only the western states. "A major general who was in the prime of life—who had fought with reputation under WAYNE—who had signalized his name and character in the memorable and well contested events at Tippecanoe and Fort Meigs; and who had, by a bloodless victory on the Thames, achieved by the suggestions of his masterly genius, given peace to a widely extended frontier; restored an important territory to our government, and acquired possession of the greater portion of Upper Canada, was thus directed to remain in a district at no one point of which was there more than a regiment stationed."

"In the meantime the Secretary had ventured on the very indelicate and outrageous proceeding of not only designating a subordinate officer for a particular service, within the district, but of transmitting the order directly to him to take a certain portion of the troops, without consulting the commanding officer of the immediate post or district. His order of the 25th of April to Major HOLMES, was not less insulting to the commanding general, than it was conducive to every species of insubordination. The command of a major general was not even nominal, if a secretary at a distance of one thousand miles, were permitted thus to interfere in the internal concerns of his district.

"This course was evidently intended as a source of mortification to General HARRISON, when contrasted with the unlimited powers confided to him in the campaigns of 1812-13. On the receipt, therefore, of the notification from the War Department, of the order of the 25th of April, General HARRISON instantly addressed a letter of resignation to the Secretary, and a notification of it to the President. As soon as Governor SHELBY heard of the resignation of General Harrison, he lost no time in addressing the President in his usual forcible terms, to prevent his acceptance of it; but unfortunately for the public interest the President was on a visit to Virginia, to which place the letters from General HARRISON and Governor SHELBY were forwarded, and that of the latter was not received until after Secretary ARMSTRONG, *without the previous consent of the President*, had assumed to himself the high prerogative of accepting the resignation. The President expressed his great regret that the letter of Governor SHELBY had not been received earlier, as in that case the valuable services of General HARRISON would have been preserved to the nation in the ensuing campaign."[50]

In 1813, Commodore PERRY wrote to General HARRISON—"You know what has been my opinion as to the future Commander-in-chief of the army. I pride myself not a little, I assure you, on seeing my predictions so near being verified; yes, my dear friend, I expect to hail you as the chief who is to redeem the honor of our arms in the North."

At a skirmish with the Indians at Chatham, before the battle of the Thames, PERRY remonstrated with HARRISON upon his exposure, when the latter replied, that "it was necessary that a general should set an example."

In 1814, General MCARTHUR wrote to General HARRISON;—"You, sir, stand the highest with the militia of this state of *any* general in the service, and I am confident that no man can fight them to so great an advantage; and I think their extreme solicitude may be the means of calling you to this frontier."

On being asked how he gained the control and confidence of the militia, he replied—"By treating them with affection and kindness—by always recollecting that they were my fellow-citizens, whose feelings I was bound to respect, and by sharing on every occasion the hardships which they were obliged to undergo."

Here ended General HARRISON's brilliant and glorious military career. For nearly a quarter of a century he had been a prominent actor in the battles of his country—had lead his countrymen through every danger, and in the language of the present Vice President of the United States, "had never sustained a defeat." When he could no longer serve his country in the field, he gave up his command and retired to private life.[51]

---

[50] Dawson's Life of Harrison.

[51] If General Harrison had not been a disinterested and high-minded man—if he could have sacrificed his sense of duty to pecuniary considerations, he might have remained with his family, enjoying his high rank, and its emoluments, and reposing upon his laurels; but he disdained command, or the reception of pay for services which he was not permitted to perform, and cheerfully retired to private life when he could no longer be useful in the field.—*Judge Hall.*

CHAPTER XXVI.

Harrison elected to Congress—Vote of thanks and a gold medal presented—Opinion of Colonel Johnson—Harrison's militia bill.

IN 1814, General HARRISON was appointed, with Governor SHELBY and General CASS, to treat with the western Indians; and after the peace with Great Britain, 1815, he was placed at the head of another commission, associated with General MCARTHUR and the Hon. JOHN GRAHAM. Under both these appointments, satisfactory treaties were concluded—the former at Greenville, and the latter at Detroit.

In 1816, he was elected to fill a vacancy in the House of Representatives in Congress, occasioned by the resignation of the Hon. JOHN MCLEAN, and also for two years succeeding. There were six candidates, and he received one thousand majority over all. At this session, a resolution was introduced, presenting the thanks of Congress, and directing medals to be struck, to be given to General HARRISON and Governor SHELBY. When the resolution came before the Senate, MR. LACOCK moved to strike out the name of General HARRISON, and the motion was carried—Yeas 13, Nays 11.[52]

About the same time, one of the contractors of the army, whose profits had been diminished by the integrity of HARRISON, charged him with improper conduct while commanding the army. The General demanded an investigation, and it was while this was pending that MR. LACOCK made the ungenerous motion, which gave a blow to the intrepid hero most unjust, and which he felt to be unmerited. Yet, disgraceful as was this procedure, in his own words, "his respect for Congress would not permit him to impugn its motives."[53] This magnanimity under such stinging circumstances cannot be

---

[52] Niles' Register.
[53] General Harrison, in a letter upon the subject of Mr. Lacock's motion, dated July 16, 1816, used the following language:—'A vote of the Senate of the United States has attached to my name a disgrace which I am fully convinced no time or no effort of mine will ever be able to efface. Their censure is indeed negative, but it is not on that account the less severe.

too highly extolled. But we must let facts speak for themselves, and when we have given them, we shall leave the reader to make up his own mind who was honored and applauded, and who disgraced and contemned. The following is extracted from the Journal of the House of Representatives, Thursday, January 23, 1817:—

"Mr. JOHNSON of Kentucky,[54] from the committee to which was referred the letter and report of the acting Secretary of War, on the application of General WILLIAM H. HARRISON respecting his expenditures of public money while commanding the north-western army, made a report thereon, stating that the committee are unanimously of opinion that General HARRISON stands above suspicion as to his having had any pecuniary or improper connexion with the officers of the commissariat for the supply of his army; that he did not wantonly or improperly interfere with the rights of the contractors; and that in his whole conduct, as the commander of the said army, he was governed by a laudable zeal for and devotion to, the public service and interest; which said report was read and considered.

Colonel JOHNSON again stated that General HARRISON "stood above suspicion, and was in his measures governed by a proper zeal and devotion to the public interest." MR. HULBERT, also on the committee, stated, that he had been prejudiced against General HARRISON, but that the investigation had satisfied him that the accusation was false and cruel. "In a word," said MR. H., "I feel myself authorized to say, that every member of the committee is fully

---

Could a vote positively expressing my unworthiness, attach to me more obloquy than one which declares that I am the only man of the army which I commanded, who did not deserve the thanks of the nation. Could anything but cowardice or treason justify this excessive rigor!—and yet it is not pretended that I am guilty of either. What then is my crime, and what the reasons upon which the vote of the Senate was justified? Why an investigation before the House of Representatives was pending, solicited by myself and some one or more persons, had impressed every member of Congress to whom I was unknown, with the belief that I deserved no merit for the success of the campaign, and that I was forced against my inclination to pursue the British army. My respect for the first branch of the Legislature of my country, will not permit me to impugn its motives. I am bound to believe that the majority at least acted from correct principles; but on a subject so important to an individual; upon a vote which was to attach disgrace to his character, which will follow him to his grave, and which will cause the blush to raise upon the cheek of his children, should they not have paused?"

[54] Colonel Richard M. Johnson, who was chairman of the committee appointed at the request of General Harrison, to investigate the charge against him.

satisfied, that the conduct of General HARRISON, in relation to the subject matter of this inquiry, has been that of a brave, honest, and honorable man; and that, instead of deserving censure, he merits the thanks and applause of his country."

On the 24th of March, 1818, MR. DICKERSON brought the subject again before the Senate. In his introductory remarks, the mover said, there was an objection to a similar resolution offered two years before, and that was, the investigation then pending before the House. Nothing could be done until the committee of investigation had reported, and no report was made until the 23d of January, 1817. The session terminating soon after, left no opportunity for the passage of the resolution. MR. DICKERSON then offered the following:—

"*Resolved* by the Senate and House of Representatives of the United States of America, in Congress assembled, That the thanks of Congress be, and they are hereby, presented to Major General WILLIAM HENRY HARRISON and ISAAC SHELBY, late Governor of Kentucky, and through them to the officers and men under their command, for their gallantry and good conduct in defeating the combined British and Indian forces under Major General PROCTOR, on the Thames, in Upper Canada, on the 5th of October, 1813, capturing the British army with the baggage, camp equipage and artillery; and that the President of the United States be requested to cause two gold medals to be struck, emblematical of this triumph, and presented to General HARRISON and ISAAC SHELBY, late Governor of Kentucky."

MR. DICKERSON then spoke at some length upon the subject. One objection to the passage of the first resolution in 1816, was, that it was charged that HARRISON would not have followed PROCTOR had it not been for Governor SHELBY. In alluding to this, MR. DICKERSON said:—"SHELBY, generous as he is brave, disclaims this exclusive merit, and in a letter, which I beg leave to read, denies, in the most positive terms, having used the language ascribed to him: and he gives to General HARRISON the highest praise for his promptitude and vigilance in pursuing PROCTOR; for the skill with which he arranged his troops for meeting the enemy, and for his distinguished bravery during the battle.

"He states that the duties of General HARRISON, as Commander-in-chief of the north-western army, were in the highest degree arduous; and that such was the zeal and fidelity with which they were performed, they could not have been committed to better hands. Of these particulars no one could know better: no one would judge better than Governor SHELBY. I have many other documents and papers to show that Governor SHELBY was not mistaken in the statements he has made, and which I will read, if any doubt should be expressed upon this subject. I trust, however, that no such doubt will be entertained, and am confident that honorable gentlemen will feel a pleasure in awarding to General HARRISON that testimony of applause, which a sense of duty induced them formerly to withhold."

The resolution passed the Senate *unanimously* on the 30th of March, and the *same day* went through three readings in the House, and passed, with only one dissentient voice.[55]

General HARRISON had gained his battles by the militia, and his own skill in training and manœuvring them. The adoption of an efficient militia system was one object which induced him to accept the nomination for Congress. Another was the relief of the soldiers who served in the two wars. He soon reported a militia bill and an explanatory report.[56] The plan was highly approved by MR. MONROE and MR. CRAWFORD. The latter, doubting the constitutionality of such a system, drew up an amendment to the constitution to embrace it; but, having just finished a war, the members were tired of military details, and refused to adopt a plan which would have silenced all disputes about situations in the military college, and by which the children of the rich and poor would have received the same education. The General supported his bill with a speech, and MR. WILLIAMS, of North Carolina, afterward said, in alluding to it, "The gentleman from Ohio has depicted the dangers of a standing army to a government like ours, in a strain of eloquence such as has rarely been witnessed in this House."

---

[55] See Journals of the Senate and House of Representatives, for 1818.

[56] The plan proposed in the Report, and supported by Mr. H., was that of the ancient republics, which mingled military instruction with the ordinary education of youth, commencing with the elementary military duties at the primary schools, and ending with the higher tactics act the colleges. The expense was to be borne by the United States; but to obviate the objection of the increase of patronage which it would give to the general government, the instructors were to be appointed by the states respectively.—*Judge Hall.*

CHAPTER XXVII.

General Harrison in Congress—In the Senate of Ohio—Censure for his vote upon the bill for the punishment of criminals—His letter on the subject.

IN 1818, General HARRISON introduced in the House a resolution in honor of the memory of KOSCIUSKO, and made a classic and touching speech. He was an ardent advocate for the acknowledgment of the independence of the South American republic. Upon the resolution to censure General JACKSON for his conduct during the Seminole war, General HARRISON delivered an eloquent address to the House. While he disapproved of one act, he applauded the patriotism of the hero of New Orleans, and gave him full and open credit for his many good deeds.[57]

In 1819, General HARRISON was elected a member of the Senate of Ohio. Here he served two years, devoting all the energies of his gigantic mind to his public duties; and during this time, as an elector for president and vice-

---

[57] General Harrison concluded his remarks, thus—"If the resolutions pass, I would address him" (General Jackson) "thus: 'In the performance of a sacred duty imposed by their construction of the constitution, the representatives of the people have found it necessary to disapprove a single act of your brilliant career; they have done it in the full conviction that the hero who has guarded her rights in the field, will bow with reverence to the civil institutions of his country—that he has admitted as his creed, that the character of the soldier can never be complete without eternal reference to the character of the citizen. Your country has done for you all that a country can do for the most favored of her sons. The age of deification is past; it was an age of tyranny and barbarism: the adoration of man should be addressed to his Creator alone. You have been feasted in the Pritanes of the cities. Your statue shall be placed in the capitol, and your name be found in the songs of the virgins. Go, gallant chief, and bear with you the gratitude of your country. Go, under the full conviction, that as her glory is identified with yours, she has nothing more dear to her but her laws, nothing more sacred but her constitution. Even an unintentional error shall be sanctified to her service. It will teach posterity that the government which could disapprove the conduct of a Marcellus, will have the fortitude to crush the vices of a Marius.'

These sentiments, sir, lead to results in which all must unite. General Jackson will still live in the hearts of his fellow-citizens, and the constitution of your country will be immortal."

president, be voted for JAMES MONROE and DANIEL D. TOMPKINS. He was subsequently chosen an elector, and voted for HENRY CLAY.

During the time he was in the Senate of Ohio, a bill was introduced for the punishment of offences against the state. It contained a clause by which persons fined for *criminal* offences, were to be apprenticed to respectable citizens for sufficient sums to pay the fines. In this shape it passed the House almost unanimously. In the Senate a motion was made and carried to strike out the clause alluded to, and General HARRISON, with 11 other senators,[58] voted to *retain* the clause, "as the most mild and human mode of dealing with the offenders for whose cases it was intended." In the Hamilton (Butler County, Ohio) Intelligencer, of December 15th, 1821, a writer endeavored to misrepresent the vote of the minority of the Senate, and to lead the reader to imagine that persons imprisoned for mere debt, were to be treated as criminals, and so apprenticed. When the article in the Intelligencer fell under the eye of General HARRISON, he immediately wrote the following letter to the editor, and it appeared in his paper of December of 31st, 1821.

"Sir: In your paper of the 15th instant, I observed a most violent attack upon eleven other members of the late Senate and myself, for a supposed vote given at the last session for the passage of a law to 'sell debtors in certain cases.' If such had been our conduct I acknowledge that we should not only deserve the censure which the writer has bestowed on us, but the execration of every honest man in society. An act of that kind is not only opposed to the principles of justice and humanity, but would be a palpable violation of the constitution of the State, which every legislator is sworn to support; and sanctioned by a House of Representatives and 12 Senators, it would indicate a state of depravity which would fill every patriotic bosom with the most alarming anticipations. But the fact is, that no such proposition was ever made in the legislature or even thought of. The act to which the writer alludes has no more relation to the collection of 'debts' than it has to the discovery of longitude. It was an act for the punishment

---

[58] Among those who voted for the law beside General Harrison, were Eli Baldwin, Esq., who was the administration candidate for the gubernatorial chair of Ohio, in 1836, and the Hon. Thomas Morris, one of the present administration senators from Ohio in Congress, and all the members of the Ohio House of Representatives from the county of Hamilton. *See Journals of the Senate and House of Representatives, of Ohio.*

of offences against the State, and that part of which has so deeply wounded the feelings of your correspondent, was passed by the House of Representatives and voted for by the 12 senators under the impression that it was the most mild and human mode of dealing with the offenders for whose cases it was intended. It was adopted by the House of Representatives as a part of the general system of criminal law, which was then undergoing a complete revision and amendment; the necessity of this is evinced by the following facts:—For several years past, it had become apparent that the Penitentiary system was becoming more and more burdensome at every session; a large appropriation was called for to meet the excess of expenditure above the receipts of the establishment. In the commencement of the session of 1820, the deficit amounted to near $20,000.

This growing evil required the immediate interposition of some vigorous legislative measure; two were recommended as being likely to produce the effect;—first, placing the institution under better management, and secondly, lessening the number of convicts who were sentenced for short periods and whose labor was found of course to be most unproductive. In pursuance of the latter principle, thefts to the amount of $50, or upwards, were subjected to punishment in the Penitentiary, instead of $10 which was the former minimum sum—this was easily done. But the great difficulty remained to determine what should be the punishment of those numerous larcenies below the sum of $50. By some, whipping was proposed, by others punishment by hard labor in the county jails, and by others it was thought best to make them work on the highways.

To all these, there appeared insuperable objections: fine and imprisonment was adopted by the House of Representatives as the only alternative, and as it was well known these vexatious pilferings were generally perpetrated by the most worthless vagabonds in society, it was added that when they could not pay the fines and costs which are always part of the sentence and punishment, that their services should be sold out to any person who would pay their fine and costs for them. This was the clause which was passed, as I believe, by a unanimous vote of the House, and stricken out in the Senate in opposition of the 12 who have been denominated. A little further trouble in examining the journals would have shown your correspondent that this was considered as a substitute for whipping, which was lost in the Senate, and in the House by a small majority, after being once passed.

I think, Mr. Editor, I have said enough to show that this obnoxious law would not have applied to 'unfortunate debtors of 64 years,' but to infamous offenders, who depredate upon the property of their fellow-citizens, and who by the constitution of the State as well as the principle of existing laws, were subject to involuntary servitude. I must confess I had no very sanguine expectations of beneficial effect from this measure, as it would apply to convicts who had attained the age of maturity. But I had supposed that a woman or a youth who, convicted of an offence, and remained in jail for the payment of the fine and costs imposed, might with great advantage be transferred to the residence of some decent, virtuous, private family, whose precept and example would gently lead them back to the paths of virtue. I would appeal to the candor of your correspondent to say whether if there were an individual confined under the circumstances I have mentioned, for whose fate he was interested, he would not gladly see him transferred, from the filthy inclosure of a jail, and the still more filthy inhabitants, to the comfortable mansion of some virtuous citizen, whose admonitions would check his vicious propensities and whose authority over him would be no more than is exercised over thousands of apprentices in our country; and those bound servants which are tolerated in our, as well as every other State in the Union. Far from advocating the abominable principles attributed to me by your correspondent, I think that imprisonment for debt, under any circumstances but that where fraud is alleged, is at war with the best principles of our constitution, and ought to be abolished.

I am, Sir, your humble servant,

WM. H. HARRISON.

North Bend, 22d December, 1821.

CHAPTER XXVIII.

The Missouri restriction—Harrison elected United States Senator—Public acts—Appointed Minister to Colombia —Treatment upon his recall—Is a Candidate for the Presidency in 1836—again nominated in 1839, for the same office.

IN 1822, General HARRISON was a candidate for Congress, but lost his election in consequence of having voted against the Missouri restriction. In February, 1819, when he was a member of the House of Representatives, a law was passed authorizing the Missouri Territory to form a state constitution.

General JAMES TALLMADGE, then a member from New York, moved the following amendment:—"Provided, that the further introduction of Slavery or involuntary servitude be prohibited, (in the new state,) except for the punishment of crimes, whereof the party shall have been fully convicted." 2d. "That all children born within said state after the admission thereof into the Union, shall be free at the age of 25 years."

"On these amendments," says NILES, "a long and spirited debate ensued. The southern and most of the western members warmly opposed these amendments, as having a direct tendency to break up the compact of the Union between the states, and destroy that provision in the federal constitution, which secures slave property to those states that choose to hold it. General HARRISON voted against any restriction on the new state, but it was carried in the House, yeas 87, nays 78."

The Senate struck out these respective clauses, and the convention of Missouri was left free and unshackled in the formation of the state constitution. The next year, when the state of Missouri applied for admission into the Union, as a slave state, the same restriction was again attempted, but finally, through the matchless abilities and exertions of HENRY CLAY, she was admitted into the Union, free of restriction.

It was the wish of General HARRISON to leave the Missouri convention as free as the constitution of the United States would allow, and to put no restrictions upon the new state which had not been placed on others. His vote was in accordance with his strict construction of the federal constitution, and his earnest desire to put Missouri on an equality with her older sisters of the Union. When he was defeated in 1822, the National Intelligencer, (Oct. 30, 1822,) used the following language:—

"A friend informs us, which we are sorry to learn, that General Harrison was opposed, as a friend to the general government, but *particularly* on account of his adherence to that principle of the constitution *which secures to the people of the south their pre-existing rights.*"

In 1824, General HARRISON was elected to the Senate of the United States, and, as chairman of the military committee,[59] introduced a bill to prevent desertion in the army. His plan was to raise the character of the officers and to hold out inducements to soldiers to perform their duties. He likewise brought forward a bill to decrease the duty on salt, it being a necessary of life. He supported the bill to confer cadet appointments, at West Point, on the sons of those who had bravely fallen in their country's service.

His exertions in favor of pensions to old soldiers will never be forgotten. With all his masterly powers he supported the bill introduced by the excellent BLOOMFIELD, and which was the means of rescuing many a deserving and brave man from want and neglect.

In 1828, General HARRISON was appointed minister plenipotentiary to the Republic of Colombia. He embarked immediately and arrived at Maracaybo, on the 22d of December, and thence proceeded to Bogota. He found every thing in concision, and BOLIVAR much inclined to favor the military party which wished to confer upon him a dictatorship. To this the more democratic of the people were strongly opposed, and they eventually succeeded in their views. The plain appearance and republican manners of the minister, led to his being suspected, by a people ever jealous, of favoring the democratic party, and subjected him to many petty persecutions from the aristocracy, against which he gallantly sustained himself. One of JACKSON's first acts upon taking the Presidential chair, was to recall General HARRISON. Before his return however, and after he had taken his leave as minister, he addressed a letter to the Colombian hero, as a personal friend. This document,

---

[59] In place of General Jackson, who had resigned.

replete with wisdom, goodness and patriotism, will be found in our appendix, and should be carefully read and studied. It breathes the purest principles and minutely describes the truly great man.

In his recall he was treated with great rudeness, though it does not appear that the government was at fault. The sloop of war, Natchez sailed from New York, in June, 1829, and carried out his successor, and her commander. Captain CLAXTON, was ordered to stop at a certain port for the purpose of taking General HARRISON on board.[60] He had been previously notified that the vessel would be at Carthagena at a certain time, and he was to hold himself in readiness to return by her. He waited at the port for a long time, but the sloop of war did not make her appearance, although at the Island of Curracoa, only 200 miles distant, the Captain had been informed that General HARRISON was waiting at Carthagena with intense anxiety, and that he was in extremely bad health.[61] In consequence of negligence he was detained in a foreign country three months, subjected to expense, sickness and mortification. He returned in a private vessel, and, we understand, at his own expense.

Upon ascertaining the facts, the then Secretary of the Navy, was willing and urgent to pursue the course of justice in the premises, but as General HARRISON had been the only sufferer, he would not consent to it, and the Secretary yielded to his particular request to forgive and forget. In this manner has General HARRISON always met the slights of those who could not appreciate the nobility of a heart devoted wholly to his country and hid country's good.

He now retired to his farm at North Bend, and devoted himself to the cultivation of his property; living in the plain style of our old republican farmers, and enjoying the truest happiness in the bosom of an affectionate wife, and the young and lovely smiles of his children.

His farm on the Ohio river contains very superior corn ground, and some years since, when corn was low, he established a distillery, in order to convert his surplus into an article more portable and profitable. He soon, however, perceived the injurious effects resulting from such manufactories, and abolished his distillery; thus setting a bright and useful example to those

---

[60] The Globe of 1836.
[61] Washington Mirror.

around him, sacrificing his own pecuniary interest to the good of the community. In his address to the Hamilton County Agricultural Society, delivered June 16, 1831, he alluded to this subject in a neat and feeling manner, concluding thus:—"I speak more freely of the practice of converting the material of 'the staff of life' (and for which so many human beings yearly perish) into an article which is so destructive of health and happiness, because in that way I have sinned myself; *but in that way I shall sin no more.*"

In the same address, he drew the picture of a farmer in glowing and vivid colors. In the portraiture of a hero returning from the field of glory to the humble retirement of a farm, we see General HARRISON conspicuously, though unconsciously shadowed forth. An extract embracing this sketch, may be found in the appendix. At this time, he was still at his plough, earning his daily bread by the sweat of his brow, nor was he visited by the politics of the country until in 1836, when he was taken up by a portion of the states and run in opposition to MARTIN VAN BUREN, for the Presidency. There were several candidates in the field against the present executive at the same time. At the east, DANIEL WEBSTER stood prominent;—at the south, Judge WHITE;—in most of the middle and western states, General HARRISON was the candidate. It can scarcely be said that there was any concentrated action among the opposition, nor was he taken up until within a few months of the election, and yet he received seventy-two electoral votes.

On the 4th of December, 1839, a full National Whig Convention assembled at Harrisburgh, Pennsylvania, and of that body, he received the unanimous vote when nominated as the candidate of the party for the Presidency. Some months previous to this, he had been nominated as the candidate of the anti-masons, and in reply to the notification of the selection, he addressed a letter to the Hon. HARMER DENNY, in which he expressed at length his views of the character and extent of the power vested by the constitution in the President. In his reply to the communication of the committee of the convention of 4th of December, he referred to this letter to MR. DENNY, and one also written to the Hon. SHERROD WILLIAMS. We have not room for these documents, but have made extracts from the former, which will be found in the appendix, and to which the attention of the reader is directed. We have still another object in selecting but one of his letters on this subject. We are writing a historical, and not a political book. We do not omit other letters because they have any electioneering paragraphs, but that we may not, even in appearance, lean to the one side or the other. Our politics are known—we have made no secret of them, yet we disclaim all party prejudice in the present work. We speak of the public acts of General HARRISON—of the great powers conferred on him by JEFFERSON, ADAMS and MADISON. We have endeavored to exhibit without prejudice the manner in which he discharged all trusts reposed in him, and feel confident that our work cannot be called political.

He is now before the people as a candidate for the Presidency, and this we record as history.

For his views of what should be the conduct of the President of the United States, we again refer to the extracts from his letter to the Hon. HARMER DENNY. He expressly says, that he thinks a President should not serve more than one term, and in his letter to the committee of the Harrisburgh Convention, repeats his declaration, that, should he be elected, he would "under no circumstances consent to be a candidate for a second term."

The opinions and deeds of every candidate for so important an office as that of chief magistrate of this great republic, should be ever known and examined by the people. With this sentiment constantly before us, have we written this book, and the reader must judge how closely we have adhered to the guide adopted.

CHAPTER XXIX.

A retrospect of the acts and character of Harrison.

WILLIAM HENRY HARRISON entered the service of his country when quite a boy. He went immediately to the west where soldiers were wanted. He fought bravely by the side of WAYNE, and secured the repeated applause of his commander. When scarcely a man, he was made commander of Fort Washington, an exposed post, and charged with the care of transmitting arms and provisions to forts more advanced. He was appointed the first Governor of Indiana, and remained in that situation until called to the command of the north-western army. During the campaigns of 1812, 1813, he was constantly in service, and devoted his best and greatest energies to his country. He followed the British into Canada and captured the whole army of PROCTOR. He was then hailed as the WASHINGTON of the west, and on his journey to the capitol, was greeted with the most enthusiastic rejoicings. On his way, a public dinner was given him at Tammany Hall, New York, under the direction of the Republican General Committee, at which 300 persons sat down. The venerable patriot, Colonel RUTGERS, presided, assisted by four vice presidents.

Subsequently, as member of Congress, member of the Ohio Legislature, and minister to Colombia, he was still more distinguished than as a warrior;—his civil exertions for his country even exceeded his glory in the field. He was always with the people, and in favor of placing as much power as possible directly in their hands.

"When high in civil office, he never forgot his responsibility to the people, nor abused the great powers with which he was intrusted. When placed at the head of the army, he was neither violent nor arbitrary. He never rashly exposed the lives of his men in battle, for the selfish purpose of winning laurels to deck his own brow. He never crushed others, that he might stride into power himself. He never set aside the laws of his country, nor insulted the majesty of the people in the persons of their officers. He was a brave soldier, without being a violent man; an accomplished leader, without inordinate ambition; a conqueror, without forgetting the precepts of justice and mercy."[62]

Retired to private life, he lived and still lives as a plain, republican farmer. Some years since he was appointed clerk of the Hamilton County Court, and he still fills that office. He was also chosen President of the Hamilton County Agricultural Society, which station he occupied with great credit to himself, and benefit to the association.

A gentleman who wrote recently to the author, describes General HARRISON as being daily engaged in the labor of his farm, and attending personally to the fulfilment of a contract he had made to deliver a large quantity of stone for a public work in the neighborhood. He is remarkable for his true Virginian hospitality, and his table, instead of being covered with exciting wines, is well supplied with the best cider.

Before closing this, our last chapter, we must refer to one circumstance, which has been denied by some of his friends, though there certainly was no necessity for such denial. We allude to his reception at Philadelphia, in 1836. Thousands and tens of thousands crowded Chesnut street wharf upon his arrival, and greeted him with continual cheering as he landed. He stepped into the barouche, but the crowd pressed forward so impetuously, that the horses became frightened and reared frequently. A rush was made to unharness the animals, when the General spoke to several, and endeavored to prevent it; but the team was soon unmanageable, and it became necessary to take them off. A rope was brought, and attached to the carriage, by which the people drew it to the Marshall House. This act was the spontaneous burst of ten thousand grateful hearts. Pennsylvanians fought under the hero, and they loved him. We speak particularly on this point, because we were an eye-witness of all that passed. Had the horses behaved well and gently, the barouche would not have been dragged through the street by the people.

Some years since a bill was brought forward in Congress, for the relief of J. C. HARRISON, when Colonel RICHARD M. JOHNSON, of Kentucky, spoke on the subject. We conclude our labors with the following extract from this speech of the Colonel:—

---

[62] Judge Hall.

"One of the securities is General WILLIAM HENRY HARRISON—and who is Gen. HARRISON? The son of one of the signers of the Declaration of Independence, who spent the greater part of his large fortune, in redeeming the pledge he then gave of his 'fortune, life, and sacred honor,' to secure the liberties of his country.

"Of the career of Gen. HARRISON I need not speak—the history of the west is *his* history. For forty years he has been identified with its interests, its perils, and its hopes. Honored and beloved in the walks of peace, and distinguished by his ability in the councils of his country, he has been yet more illustriously distinguished in the field.

"During the late war, he was longer in active service than any other general officer;—he was perhaps oftener in action than any one of them, and *never sustained a defeat.*"[63]

---

[63] See Journals of the House of Representatives for 1831. Also, many points stated in this chapter, will be found fully substantiated by various articles in the appendix.

APPENDIX.

CORRESPONDENCE BETWEEN GENERAL WAYNE AND MAJOR CAMPBELL.

I.

MIAMIS RIVER, Aug. 21, 1794.

SIR,

An army of the United States of America, said to be under your command, having taken post on the banks of the Miamis, for upwards of the last twenty-four hours, almost within the reach of the guns of this fort, being a post belonging to His Majesty the King of Great Britain, occupied by His Majesty's troops, and which I have the honor to command, it becomes me to inform myself, as speedily as possible, in what light I am to view your making such near approaches to this garrison.

I have no hesitation on my part to say, that I know of no war existing between Great Britain and America.

I have the honor to be, &c.

WILLIAM CAMPBELL,
Major 24th Reg't, commanding a British post on the banks of the Miamis.

To Major General Wayne, &c. &c.

II.

CAMP ON THE BANKS OF THE MIAMIS,
August 21, 1794.

SIR,

I have received your letter of this date, requiring from me the motives which have moved the army under my command to the position they at present occupy, far within the acknowledged jurisdiction of the United States of America.

Without questioning the authority, or the propriety, sir, of your interrogatory, I think I may, without breach of decorum, observe to you, that were you entitled to an answer, the most full and satisfactory one was announced to you from the muzzles of my small arms yesterday morning in the action against hordes of savages in the vicinity of your post, which terminated gloriously to the American arms. But had it continued until the Indians, &c. were driven under the influence of the post and guns you mention, they would not have much impeded the progress of the victorious army under my command; as no such post was established at the commencement of the present war between the Indians and the United States.

I have the honor to be, sir, &c.

ANTHONY WAYNE,
Major General and Commander-in-chief of
the Federal army.

To Major Wm. Campbell, &c.

III.

Fort Miamis, Aug. 22, 1794.

Sir,

Although your letter of yesterday's date fully authorizes me to any act of hostility against the army of the United States of America in this neighborhood under your command, yet, still anxious to prevent that dreadful decision, which perhaps is not intended to be appealed to by either of our countries, I have forborne for these two days past to resent those insults which you have offered to the British flag flying at this fort, by approaching it within pistol-shot of my works, not only singly, but in numbers, with arms in their hands.

Neither is it my wish to wage war with individuals. But should you after this continue to approach my post in the threatening manner you are at this moment doing, my indispensable duty to my King and Country, and the honor of my profession, will oblige me to have recourse to those measures which thousands of either nation may hereafter have cause to regret, and which I solemnly appeal to God I have used my utmost endeavors to arrest.

I have the honor to be, sir, &c.

WM. CAMPBELL.

To Major General Wayne, &c.

[No other notice was taken of this letter than what is expressed in the following letter. The fort and works were however reconnoitered in every direction, at some points possibly within pistol-shot. It was found to be a regular, strong work, the front covered by a wide river, with four guns mounted in that face. The rear, which was the most susceptible of approach, had two regular bastions furnished with eight pieces of artillery, the whole surrounded with a wide, deep ditch. From the bottom of the ditch to the top of the parapet, was about twenty feet perpendicular. The works were also surrounded by an abbatis, and furnished with a strong garrison.]

IV.

CAMP ON THE BANKS OF THE MIAMIS,
August 22, 1794.

SIR,

In your letter of the 21st instant you declare, "I have no hesitation on my part to say that I know of no war existing between Great Britain and America."

I, on my part, declare the same; and the only cause I have to entertain a contrary idea at present is, the hostile act you are now in commission of,— that is, recently taking post far within the well-known and acknowledged limits of the United States, and erecting a fortification in the heart of the settlements of the Indian tribes now at war with the United States.

This, sir, appears to be an act of the highest aggression, and destructive to the peace and interest of the Union. Hence, it becomes my duty to desire, and I do hereby desire and demand, in the name of the President of the United States, that you immediately desist from any further act of hostility or aggression, by forbearing to fortify, and by withdrawing the troops, artillery, and stores under your orders and direction, forthwith, and removing to the nearest port occupied by His Britannic Majesty's troops at the peace of

1783—and which you will be permitted to do unmolested by the troops under my command.

I am, sir, with very great respect, &c.

ANTHONY WAYNE.

To Major William Campbell, &c.

V.

Fort Miamis, Aug. 22, 1794.

Sir,

I have this moment the honor to acknowledge the receipt of your letter of this date. In answer to which I have only to say, that being placed here in the command of a British post, and acting in a military capacity only, I cannot enter into any discussion either on the right or impropriety of my occupying my present position. Those are matters that I conceive will be best left to the ambassadors of our different nations.

Having said this much, permit me to inform you, that I certainly will not abandon this post at the summons of any power whatever, until I receive orders from those I have the honor to serve under, or the fortune of war should oblige me.

I must still adhere, sir, to the purport or my letter this morning, to desire that your army, or individuals belonging to it, will not approach within reach of my cannon without expecting the consequences attending it.

Although I have said in the former part of my letter, that my situation here is totally military, yet let me add, sir, that I am much deceived if His Majesty, the King of Great Britain, had not a post on this river at and prior to the period you mention.

I have the honor to be, &c.

WM. CAMPBELL,
Major of the 24th Regiment, commanding at Fort Miamis.
To Major General Wayne, &c.

[The only notice taken of this letter, was in immediately setting fire to and destroying every thing within view of the fort, and even under the muzzles of the guns.]

Boston Chronicle, Oct. 13, 1794.

MISCHECANOCQUAH TO GOVERNOR HARRISON.

FORT WAYNE, Jan. 25, 1812.

GOVERNOR HARRISON,

My friend—I have been requested by my nation to speak to you, and I obey their request with pleasure, because I believe their situation requires all the aid I can afford them.

When your speech by Mr. Dubois was received by the Miamies, they answered it, and I made known to you their opinion at that time.

Your letter to William Wells of the 23d November last, has been explained to the Miamies and Eel-River tribes of Indians.

My friend—Although neither of these tribes have had any thing to do with the late unfortunate affair which happened on the Wabash, still they all rejoice to hear you say, that if those foolish Indians which were engaged in that action, would return to their several homes and remain quiet, that they would be pardoned, and again received by the President as his children. We believe there is none of them that will be so foolish, as not to accept of this friendly offer; whilst, at the same time, I assure you, that nothing shall be wanting on my part, to prevail on them to accept it.

All the prophet's followers have left him, (with the exception of two camps of his own tribe.) Tecumseh has just joined him with eight men only. No danger can be apprehended from them at present. Our eyes will be constantly kept on them, and should they attempt to gather strength again, we will do all in our power to prevent it, and at the same time give you immediate information of their intentions.

We are sorry that the peace and friendship which has so long existed between me red and white people, could not be preserved, without the loss of so many good men as fell on both sides in the late action on the Wabash; but we are satisfied that it will be the means of making that peace which ought to exist between us, more respected, both by the red and the white people.

We have been lately told, by different Indians from that quarter, that yon wished the Indians from this country to visit you: this they will do with pleasure when you give them information of it in writing.

My friend!—The clouds appear to be rising in a different quarter, which threatens to turn our light into darkness. To prevent this, it may require the united efforts of us all. We hope that none of us will be found to shrink from the storm that threatens to burst upon our nations.

Your friend,
MISCHECANOCQUAH,
or LITTLE TURTLE.

For the Miami and Eel-River tribes of Indians.
Witness,

WM. TURNER, *Surgeon's Mate, U. S. Army.*

I certify that the above is a true translation.

W. WELLS.

MR. EUSTIS TO GENERAL HARRISON.

WAR DEPARTMENT, Sept. 17, 1812.

SIR,

The President is pleased to assign to you the command of the north-western army, which, in addition to the regular troops and rangers in that quarter, will consist of the volunteers and militia of Kentucky, Ohio, and three thousand from Virginia and Pennsylvania, making your whole force ten thousand men.

Having provided for the protection of the western frontier, you will retake Detroit, and with a view to the conquest of Upper Canada, you will penetrate that country as far as the force under your command will, in your judgment, justify.

Every exertion is making to give you a train of artillery from Pittsburgh; to effect which, yon must be sensible, requires time. Major Stoddard, the senior officer of artillery at that place, will advise you of his arrangements and progress, and receive your instructions. Captain Gratiot, of the engineers, will report himself to you, from Pittsburgh: he will receive your orders, and join you with the first piece of artillery which can be prepared, or receive such orders as you may direct. Major Ball, of the 2d regiment of dragoons, will also report himself, and join you immediately. Such staff officers as you may appoint conformably to law, will be approved by the President.

Copies of all contracts for supplying provisions have been transmitted. Mr. Denny, the contractor at Pittsburgh, is instructed to furnish magazines of provisions at such places as you may direct.

The deputy quarter-master at Pittsburgh will continue to forward stores and munitions of every kind, and will meet your requisitions.

Colonel Buford, deputy commissary, at Lexington, is furnished with funds, and is subject to your orders. Should an additional purchasing commissary become necessary, you will appoint one, and authorize him to draw and sell bills on this department. It seems advisable to keep the local contractors in requisition as far as they can supply. With these objects in view, yon will command such means as may be practicable, exercise your own discretion, and act in all cases according to your own judgment.

Very respectfully, &c.
W. EUSTIS.

Brig. Gen. WM. H. HARRISON.

COLONEL JOHNSON TO GENERAL HARRISON.

CAMP AT LOWER SANDUSKY, July 4, 1813.

DEAR SIR,

I arrived at this place last evening with a part of the mounted regiment, after two days' march from Camp Meigs, leaving two companies four miles in the rear, who were unable to reach this place; besides about twenty horses left on the way, which I am in hopes will be able to get back to Camp Meigs, or come to this place in a few days, where we can keep them together, and recruit them. Having been in the most active service for upwards of forty days, and having travelled upwards of seven hundred miles, much of it forced marching, it is natural to conclude, that most of the horses are weak; and we feel great pleasure, and obligations to you, in finding your arrangements such as to enable us to recruit the horses of the regiment. To be ready to move with you to Detroit and Canada, against the enemies of our country, is the first wish of our hearts. Two great objects induced us to come—first, to be at the regaining of our own territory and Detroit, and at the taking of Malden—and secondly, *to serve under an officer in whom we have confidence.* We would not have engaged in the service without such a prospect, when we recollected what disasters have attended us for the want of good generals. We did not want to serve under cowards, drunkards, old grannies, nor traitors, *but under one who had proved himself to be wise, prudent, and brave.* The officers of the mounted regiment had some idea of addressing you on their anxiety to be a part of your army in the campaign against Canada, and of giving you a statement of the importance of having an opportunity to make the regiment efficient for such a campaign, by recruiting their horses. As to the men, they are active, healthy, and fond of service. This morning I have sent 100 on foot to scour the surrounding country; and wherever we are we wish continual service. Our regiment is about 900 strong when all together. I have left 100 at Defiance to regain some lost horses, and to guard that frontier.

You have not witnessed the opposition I encountered in raising the regiment. Every personal enemy, every traitor and tory, and your enemies, all combined—but in vain. Nothing but the hurry which attended our march prevented me from having 1,500 men. Nothing but the importance of the service which I thought we could render, would have justified my absence from the present catch-penny Congress. My enemies, your enemies, the enemies of the cause, would exult if the mounted regiment should, from any cause, be unable to carry a strong arm against the savages and British, when you strike the grand blow.

It is with diffidence I write you any thing touching military matters; but the desires of my soul, and the situation of the regiment, have induced me thus freely to express myself. In the morning we shall leave this place for Huron, ready to receive your orders, which will be always cheerfully executed at every hazard.

Your obedient servant,
RICHARD M. JOHNSON.

THE OFFICERS OF THE ARMY TO THE PUBLIC.

LOWER SENECA TOWN, Aug. 19, 1813.

"The undersigned, being the general, field, and staff officers with that portion of the north-western army under the immediate, command of General Harrison, have observed with regret and surprise that charges, as improper in the form as in the substance, have been made against the conduct of General Harrison, during the recent investment of Lower Sandusky. At another time, under ordinary circumstances, we should deem it improper and unmilitary thus publicly to give any opinion respecting the movements of the army. But public confidence in the commanding general is essential to the success of the campaign, and causelessly to withdraw or to withhold that confidence, is more than individual injustice—it becomes a serious injury to the service. A part of the force of which the American army consists, will derive its greatest strength and efficacy from a confidence in the commanding general, and from those moral causes which accompany and give energy to public opinion. A very erroneous idea, respecting the number of the troops then at the disposal of the General, has doubtless been the primary cause of these unfortunate and unfounded impressions. In that respect we have, fortunately, experienced a very favorable change. But we refer the public to the General's official report to the Secretary of War, of Major Croghan's successful defence of Lower Sandusky. In that will be found a statement of our whole disposable force; and he who believes that with such a force, and under the circumstances which then occurred. General Harrison ought to have advanced upon the enemy, must be left to correct his opinion in the school of experience. On a review of the course then adopted, we are decidedly of the opinion, that it was such as was dictated by military wisdom, and by a due regard to our own circumstances and to the situation of the enemy. The reason for this opinion, it is evidently improper now to give; but we hold ourselves ready at a future period, and when other circumstances shall have intervened, to satisfy every man of its correctness who is anxious to investigate and willing to receive the truth. And with a ready acquiescence, beyond the mere claims of military duty, we are prepared to obey a general, whose measures meet our most deliberate approbation, and merit that of his country.

LEWIS CASS, Brig. Gen. U. S. Army.
SAMUEL WELLS, Col. 17th Reg't U. S. Inf.
THOS. D. OWINGS, Col. 28th Reg't U. S. Inf.
GEORGE PAUL, Col. 17th Reg't U. S. Inf.
J. C. BARTLETT, Col. Q'r M. Gen.
JAMES V. BALL, Lieut. Col.
L. HUKILL. Maj. and Ass't Insp. Gen.
ROBERT MORRISON, Lieut. Col.

GEORGE TODD, Maj. 19th Reg't U. S. Inf.
WILLIAM TRIGG, Maj. 28th Reg't U. S. Inf.
JAMES SMILEY, Maj. 28th Reg't U. S. Inf.
RICHARD GRAHAM, Maj. 17th Reg't U. S. Inf.
GEORGE CROGHAN, Maj. 17th Reg't U. S. Inf.
E. D. WOOD, Maj. Engineers.

Major Croghan's Card.

Lower Sandusky, Aug. 27, 1813.

I have with much regret seen in some of the public prints such misrepresentations respecting my refusal to evacuate this post, as are calculated not only to injure me in the estimation of military men, but also to excite unfavorable impressions as to the propriety of General Harrison's conduct relative to this affair.

His character as a military man is too well established to need my approbation or support. But his public services entitle him at least to common justice. This affair does not furnish cause of reproach. If public opinion has been lately misled respecting his late conduct, it will require but a moment's cool, dispassionate reflection, to convince them of its propriety. THE MEASURES RECENTLY ADOPTED BY HIM, SO FAR FROM DESERVING CENSURE, ARE THE CLEAREST PROOFS OF HIS KEEN PENETRATION AND ABLE GENERALSHIP. It is true that I did not proceed immediately to execute his order to evacuate this post; but this disobedience was not, as some would wish to believe, the result of a fixed determination to maintain the post contrary to his most positive orders, as will appear from the following detail, which is given to explain my conduct.

About 10 o'clock on the morning of the 30th ultimo, a letter from the Adjutant General's office, dated Seneca Town, July 29th, 1813, was handed me by Mr. Connor, ordering me to abandon this post, burn it, and retreat that night to head quarters. On the reception of the order, I called a council of officers, in which it was determined not to abandon the place, at least until the further pleasure of the General should be known, as it was thought that an attempt to retreat in the open day, in the face of a superior force of the enemy, would be more hazardous than to remain in the fort, under all its disadvantages. I therefore wrote a letter to the General, couched in such terms as I thought were calculated to deceive the enemy, should it fall into his hands, which I thought more than probable,—as well as to inform the general, should it be so fortunate as to reach him, that I would wait to hear from him, before I should proceed to execute his order. This letter, contrary to my expectations, was received by the General, who, not knowing what reasons urged me to write in a tone so decisive, concluded very rationally that the manner of it was demonstrative of the most positive determination to disobey his order under any circumstances. I was therefore suspended from the command of the fort, and ordered to head quarters. But on explaining to the General my reason for not executing his orders, and my object in using the style I had done, he was so perfectly satisfied with the explanation, that I was immediately reinstated in the command.

It will be recollected that the order above alluded to, was written on the night previous to my receiving it—had it been delivered to me, as was intended, that night, I should have obeyed it without hesitation; its not reaching me in time was the only reason which induced me to consult my officers on the propriety of waiting the General's further orders.

It has been stated, also, that, "upon my representations of my ability to maintain the post, the General altered his determination to abandon it." This is incorrect. No such representations were ever made. And the last order I received from the General was precisely the same as that first given—viz., "That if I discovered the approach of a large British force by water, (presuming that they would bring heavy artillery,) time enough to effect a retreat, I was to do so; but if I could not retreat with safety, to defend the post to the last extremity."

A day or two before the enemy appeared before Fort Meigs, the General had reconnoitered the surrounding ground, and being informed that the hill on the opposite side of Sandusky completely commanded the fort, I offered to undertake, with the troops under my command, to remove it to that side. The General, upon reflection, thought it best not to attempt it, as he believed that if the enemy again appeared on this side of the lake, it would be before the work could be finished.

It is useless to disguise the fact, that this fort is commanded by the points of high ground around it; a single stroke of the eye made this clear to me the first time I had occasion to examine the neighborhood, with a view of discovering the relative strength and weakness of the place.

It would be insincere to say that I am not flattered by the many handsome things which have been said about the defence which was made by the troops under my command; but I desire no plaudits which are bestowed upon me at the expense of General Harrison.

I have at all times enjoyed his confidence so far as my rank in the army entitled me to it, and on proper occasions received his marked attention. I have felt the warmest attachment for him as a man, and my confidence in him as an *able commander* remains unshaken. I feel every assurance that he will at all times do me ample justice; and nothing could give me more pain than to see his enemies seize upon this occasion to deal out their unfriendly feelings and acrimonious dislike—and as long as he continues (as in my humble opinion he has hitherto done) to make the wisest arrangements and most judicious disposition which the forces under his command will justify, I shall not hesitate to unite with the army in bestowing upon him that confidence which he so richly merits, and which has on no occasion been withheld.

Your friend,
GEORGE CROGHAN,
Maj. 17th Infantry, commanding Lower Sandusky.

INDIANA LEGISLATURE AND GEN. HARRISON.

To His Excellency William Henry Harrison, Governor and Commander-in-chief in and over the Indiana Territory.

SIR,

The House of Representative of the Indiana Territory, in their own name and in behalf of their constituents, most cordially reciprocate the congratulations of your Excellency on the glorious result of the late sanguinary conflict with the Shawanee Prophet,[64] and the tribes of Indians confederated with him. When we see displayed in behalf of our country, not only the consummate abilities of the General, but the heroism of the man; and

---

[64] Battle of Tippecanoe.

when we take into view the benefits which must result to that country, from those exertions, we cannot for a moment withhold our need of applause.

GEORGE W. JOHNSTONE,
Speaker of the House of Representatives.

REPRESENTATIVE CHAMBER, Nov., 1811.

REPLY OF GENERAL HARRISON.

GENTLEMEN OF THE HOUSE OF REPRESENTATIVES,

Believing, as I do, that the highest reward which a republican soldier can receive, is the approbation of his fellow-citizens, I cannot be otherwise than highly gratified at the applause which you have been pleased to bestow on my conduct as commander of the late expedition. It has ever been my wish, gentlemen, to deserve the confidence of your constituents. To promote their welfare and happiness, has been for years the great object of my cares; and if in the late action it had pleased the Almighty to seal with my life, the victory which was to insure their safety, the sacrifice would have been cheerfully made.

WILLIAM H. HARRISON.

Communication on the Battle of Tippecanoe, in the National Intelligencer of December 3d, 1811.

"In a regular engagement the General has but to adopt his plan, and trust to the ability of his troops for the execution: but in cases of surprise, every thing depends upon his exertions. His voice and example must recall the fainting spirits of his men, and lead them to their duty. And I challenge history to produce another instance, where, after an enemy so nearly equal in number, so dreadful, and so brave as the North American savages, and they made more desperate by fanaticism, had penetrated the centre of a camp in the night, and were dealing death around, that the attacked have rallied and beat off the enemy. Indeed, few are the instances in which they have been able to effect a retreat.

'Tis said, and truly, that emergencies discover the man. And surely, surely, emergencies have discovered Governor Harrison to possess presence of mind, valor, and military skill, qualities which need the experience of a few battles only to make an able military commander."

(From the New York papers of 1813.)

DINNER IN HONOR OF GENERAL HARRISON.—A public dinner was given at Tammany Hail, in this city, under the direction and superintendence of the Republican General Committee of New York, to Major General Wm. H. Harrison. The company assembled amounted to about 300 persons.

On the exterior of the hall was placed a very elegant transparency, from the pencil of Mr. Holland. In the foreground several Indian chiefs were imploring the clemency of General Harrison. This transparency supported another, on which was inscribed

"HARRISON,"
"PERRY,"
"DON'T GIVE UP THE SHIP."

Fourteenth Toast.—The plaudits of a grateful people—The patriot hero's best reward.—Nine cheers.—Music, Harrison's March.

By General Harrison—The freedom of the seas, and the adaption by our government of that Roman maxim which secured to the citizen his inviolability.—Twelve cheers.

After Gen. Harrison had retired, the president (Col. Henry Rutgers) gave the following:—

Major Gen. Harrison—The deliverer of the western frontier.—Seventeen cheers.

GENERAL HARRISON'S MODESTY.—Mr. Ritchie, editor of the Richmond Enquirer, in his paper of Nov., 1813, in speaking of Harrison's account of the battle of the Thames, said:—

"General Harrison's detailed letter tells us of every thing we wish to know about the officers, except himself. He does justice to every one but Harrison, *and the world must therefore do justice to the man* who was too modest to be just to himself."

Extract from the President's (Madison's) Message, Dec. 7, 1813.

"The success on Lake Erie having opened a passage to the territory of the enemy, General Harrison commanding the north-western army, transferred the war thither; and rapidly pursuing the hostile troops fleeing with their savage associates, forced a general action, which quickly terminated in the capture of the British and the dispersion of the savage force. *This result is signally honorable to Major General Harrison, by whose military talents it was prepared*, and to the spirit of the volunteer militia equally brave and patriotic, who bore an interesting part in the scene."

JEFFERSON AND HARRISON.—It has been denied by some that General Harrison received office from Thomas Jefferson. On page 441, of the Executive Journal of the United States Senate, the following may be found:—

"I nominate William Henry Harrison to be Governor of the Indiana Territory, from the 13th day of May next, when his present commission will expire."

Again—

"I nominate William Henry Harrison of Indiana, to be a commissioner to enter into any treaty, or treaties which may be necessary, with any Indian tribes, north-west of the Ohio, and within the territory of the United States, on the subject of the boundary, or lands."

THOMAS JEFFERSON."

The message containing these nominations was transmitted to the Senate 3d Feb. 1803—read the 4th, and on the 8th taken up for consideration, when the two nominations, received the unanimous sanction of that honorable body.

GENERAL HARRISON TO GENERAL BOLIVAR.

BOGOTA, Sept. 27, 1829.

SIR,

If there is any thing in the style, the matter, or the object of this letter, which is calculated to give offence to your Excellency, I am persuaded you will readily forgive it, when you reflect on the motives which induced me to write it. An old soldier could possess no feelings but those of the kindest character towards one who has shed so much lustre on the profession of arms; nor can a citizen of the country of Washington cease to wish that, in

Bolivar, the world might behold another instance of the highest military attainments united with the purest patriotism, and the greatest capacity for civil government.

Such, sir, have been the fond hopes, not only of the people of the United States, but of the friends of liberty throughout the world. I will not say, that your Excellency has formed projects to defeat those hopes. But there is no doubt, that they have not only been formed, but are, at this moment, in progress to maturity, and openly avowed by those who possess your entire confidence. I will not attribute to these men impure motives; but can they be disinterested advisers? Are they not the very persons who will gain most by the proposed change?—who will, indeed, gain all that is to be gained, without furnishing any part of the equivalent? That *that*, the price of their future wealth and honors, is to be furnished exclusively by yourself? And of what does it consist? Your great character. Such an one, that, if a man were wise, and possessed of the empire of the Cæsars, in its best days, he would give all to obtain. Are you prepared to make this sacrifice, for such an object?

I am persuaded that those who advocate these measures, have never dared to induce you to adopt them, by any argument founded on your personal interests; and that, to succeed, it would be necessary to convince you that no other course remained, to save the country from the evils of anarchy. This is the question, then, to be examined.

Does the history of this country, since the adoption of the constitution, really exhibit unequivocal evidence that the people are unfit to be free? Is the exploded opinion of a European philosopher, of the last age, that "in the new hemisphere, man is a degraded being," to be renewed, and supported by the example of Colombia? The proofs should, indeed, be strong, to induce an American to adopt an opinion so humiliating.

Feeling always a deep interest in the success of the revolutions in the late Spanish America, I have never been an inattentive observer of events pending, and posterior to the achievement of its independence. In these events, I search in vain for a single fact to show that, in Colombia at least, the state of society is unsuited to the adoption of a free government. Will it be said that a free government did exist, but, being found inadequate to the objects for which it had been instituted, it has been superseded by one of a different character, with the concurrence of a majority of the people?

It is the most difficult thing in the world for me to believe that a people in the possession of their rights as freemen, would ever be willing to surrender them, and submit themselves to the will of a master. If any such instances are on record, the power thus transferred has been in a moment of extreme public danger, and then limited to a very short period. I do not think that it is by any means certain, that the majority of the French people favored the elevation of Napoleon to the throne of France. But, if it were so, how different were the circumstances of that country from those of Colombia, when the constitution of Cucuta was overthrown! At the period of the elevation of Napoleon to the first consulate, all the powers of Europe were the open or the secret enemies of France—civil war raged within her borders; the hereditary king possessed many partisans in every province; the people, continually betrayed by the factions which murdered and succeeded each other, had imbibed a portion of their ferocity, and every town and village witnessed the indiscriminate slaughter of both men and women, of all parties and principles. Does the history of Colombia, since the expulsion of the Spaniards, present any parallel to these scenes? Her frontiers have been never seriously menaced—no civil war raged—not a partisan of the former government was to be found in the whole extent of her territory—no factions contended with each other for the possession of power; the executive government remained in the hands of those to whom it had been committed by the people, in a fair election. In fact, no people ever passed from under the yoke of a despotic government, in the enjoyment of entire freedom, with less disposition to abuse their newly acquired power, than those of Colombia. They submitted, indeed, to a continuance of some of the most arbitrary and unjust features which distinguished the former government. If there was any disposition, on the part of the great mass of the people, to effect any change in the existing order of things; if the Colombian acts from the same motives and upon the same principles which govern mankind elsewhere, and in all ages, they would have desired to take from the government a part of the power, which, in their inexperience they had confided to it The monopoly of certain articles of agricultural produce, and the oppressive duty of the Alcavala, might have been tolerated, until the last of their tyrants were driven from the country. But when peace was restored, when not one enemy remained within its borders, it might reasonably have been supposed that the people would have desired to abolish these remains of arbitrary government, and substitute for them some tax more equal and accordant with republican principles.

On the contrary, it is pretended that they had become enamoured with these despotic measures, and so disgusted with the freedom they did enjoy, that they were more than willing to commit their destinies to the uncontrolled will of your Excellency. Let me assure you, sir, that these assertions will gain no credit with the present generation, or with posterity. They will demand the facts which had induced a people, by no means deficient in intelligence, so soon to abandon the principles for which they had so gallantly fought, and tamely surrender that liberty, which had been obtained at the expense of so much blood. And what facts can be produced? It cannot be said that life and property were not as well protected under the republican government, as they have ever been; nor that there existed any opposition to the constitution and laws, too strong for the ordinary powers of the government to put down.

If the insurrection of General Paez, in Venezuela, is adduced, I would ask, by what means was he reduced to obedience? Your Excellency, the legitimate head of the republic, appeared, and, in a moment, all opposition ceased, and Venezuela was restored to the republic. But, it is said, that this was effected by your personal influence, or the dread of your military talents, and that, to keep General Paez, and other ambitious chiefs, from dismembering the republic, it was necessary to invest your Excellency with the extraordinary powers you possess. There would be some reason in this, if you had refused to act without these powers; or, having acted as you did, you had been unable to accomplish any thing without them. But you succeeded completely, and there can be no possible reason assigned, why you would not have succeeded, with the same means, against any future attempt of General Paez, or any other general.

There appears, however, to be one sentiment, in which all parties unite; that is, that as matters now stand, yon alone can save the country from ruin, at least, from much calamity. They differ, however, very widely, as to the measures to be taken to put your Excellency in the way to render this important service. The lesser, and more interested party, is for placing the government in your hands for life; either with your present title, or with one which, it must be confessed, better accords with the nature of the powers to be exercised. If they adopt the less offensive title, and if they weave into their system some apparent checks to your will, it is only for the purpose of masking, in some degree, their real object; which is nothing short of the establishment of a despotism. The plea of necessity, that eternal argument of all conspirators, ancient or modern, against the rights of mankind, will be resorted to, to induce you to accede to their measures; and the unsettled state of the country, which has been designedly produced by them, will be adduced as evidence of that necessity.

There is but one way for your Excellency to escape from the snares which have been so artfully laid to entrap you, and that is, to stop short in the course which, unfortunately, has been already commenced. Every step you advance, under the influence of such councils, will make retreat more difficult, until it will become impracticable. You will be told that the intention is only to vest you with authority to correct what is wrong in the administration, and to put down the factions, and that, when the country once enjoys tranquillity, the government may be restored to the people. Delusive will be the hopes of those who rely upon this declaration. The promised hour of tranquillity will never arrive. If events tended to produce it, they would be counteracted by the government itself. It was the strong remark of a former President of the United States, that, "Sooner will the lover be contented with the first smiles of his mistress, than a government cease to endeavor to preserve and extend its powers." With whatever reluctance your Excellency may commence the career; with whatever disposition to abandon it, when the objects for which it was commenced have been obtained; when once fairly entered, yon will be borne along by the irresistible force of pride, habit of command, and, indeed, of self-preservation, and it will be impossible to recede.

But, it is said, that it is for the benefit of the people that the proposed change is to be made; and that by your talents and influence, alone, aided by unlimited power, the ambitious chiefs in the different departments are to be restrained, and the integrity of the republic preserved. I have said, and I most sincerely believe, that, from the state into which the country has been brought, that you alone can preserve it from the horrors of anarchy. But I cannot conceive that any extraordinary powers are necessary. The authority to see that the laws are executed, to call out the strength of the country, to enforce their execution, is all that is required, and is what is possessed by the Chief Magistrate of the United States, and of every other republic; and is what was confided to the executive, by the constitution of Cucuta. Would your talents or your energies be impaired in the council, or the field, or your influence lessened, when acting as the head of a republic?

I propose to examine, very briefly, the results which are likely to flow from the proposed change of government; 1st, in relation to the country; and, 2d, to yourself, personally. Is the tranquillity of the country to be secured by it? Is it possible for your Excellency to believe, that when the mask has been thrown off, and the people discover that a despotic government has been fixed upon them, that they will quietly submit to it? Will they forget the pass-word which, like the cross of fire, was the signal for rallying to oppose their former tyrants? Will the virgins, at your bidding, cease to chaunt the songs of liberty, which so lately animated the youth to victory? Was the patriotic blood of Colombia, all expended in the fields of Vargas, Bayaca, and Carebobo? The schools may cease to enforce upon their pupils the love of country, drawn from the examples of Cato and the Bruti, Harmodius and Aristogiton; but the glorious example of patriotic devotion, exhibited in your own Hacienda, will supply their place. Depend on it, sir, that the moment which shall announce the continuance of arbitrary power in your hands, will be the commencement of commotions which will require all your talents and energies to suppress. You may succeed. The disciplined army, at your disposal, may be too powerful for an unarmed, undisciplined, and scattered population; but one unsuccessful effort will not content them, and your feelings will be eternally racked by being obliged to make war upon those who have been accustomed to call you their father, and to invoke blessings on your head, and for no cause but their adherence to principles which you yourself had taught them to regard more than their lives.

If by the strong government which the advocates for the proposed change so strenuously recommend, one without responsibility is intended, which may put men to death, and immure them in dungeons, without trial, and one where the army is everything, and the people nothing, I must say, that, if the tranquillity of Colombia is to be preserved in this way, the wildest anarchy would be preferable. Out of that anarchy a better government might arise; but the chains of military despotism once fastened upon a nation, ages might pass away before they could be shaken off.

But I contend that the strongest of all governments is that which is most free. We consider that of the United States as the strongest, precisely because it is the most free. It possesses the faculties, equally to protect itself from foreign force or internal convulsion. In both, it has been sufficiently tried. In no country upon earth, would an armed opposition to the laws be sooner or more effectually put down. Not so much by the terrors of the guillotine and the gibbet, as from the aroused determination of the nation, exhibiting their strength, and convincing the factions that their cause was hopeless. No, sir, depend upon it, that the possession of arbitrary power, by the government of Colombia, will not be the means of securing its tranquillity; nor will the danger of disturbances solely arise from the opposition of the people. The power and the military force which it will be necessary to put in the hands of the governors of the distant provinces, added to the nature of the country, will continually present to those officers the temptation, and the means of revolt.

Will the proposed change restore prosperity to the country? With the best intentions to do so, will you be able to recall commerce to its shores and give new life to the drooping state of agriculture? The cause of the constant decline, in these great interests, cannot be mistaken. It arises from the fewness of those who labor, and the number of those who are to be supported by that labor. To support a swarm of luxurious and idle monks, and an army greatly disproportioned to the resources of the country, with a body of officers in a tenfold decree disproportioned to the army, every branch of industry is oppressed with burdens which deprive the ingenious man of the profits of his ingenuity, and the laborer of his reward. To satisfy the constant and pressing demands which are made upon it, the treasury siezes upon every thing within its grasp—destroying the very germ of future prosperity. Is there any prospect that these evils will cease with the proposed change? Can the army be dispensed with? Will the influence of the monks be no longer necessary? Believe me, sir, that the support which the government derives from both these sources, will be more than ever requisite.

But the most important inquiry is, the effect which this strong government is to have upon the people themselves. Will it tend to improve and elevate their character, and fit them for the freedom which it is pretended is to be ultimately bestowed upon them? The question has been answered from the age of Homer. Man does not learn under oppression those noble qualities and feelings which fit him for the enjoyment of liberty.

Nor is despotism the proper school in which to acquire the knowledge of the principles of republican government. A government whose revenues are derived from diverting the very sources of wealth from its subjects, will not find the means of improving the morals and enlightening the minds of the youth, by supporting systems of liberal education; and, if it could, it would not.

In relation to the effect which this investment of power is to have upon your happiness and your fame, will the pomp and glitter of a court, and the flattery of venal courtiers, reward you for the troubles and anxieties attendant upon the exercise of sovereignty, everywhere, and those which will flow from your peculiar situation? Or power, supported by the bayonet, for that willing homage which you were wont to receive from your fellow-citizens? The groans of a dissatisfied and oppressed people will penetrate the inmost recesses of your palace, and you will be tortured by the reflection, that you no longer possess that place in their affections, which was once your pride and your boast, and which would have been your solace under every reverse of fortune. Unsupported by the people, your authority can be maintained, only, by the terrors of the sword and the scaffold. And have these ever been successful under similar circumstances? Blood may smother, for a period, but can never extinguish, the fire of liberty, which you have contributed so much to kindle, in the bosom of every Colombian.

I will not urge, as an argument, the personal dangers to which you will be exposed. But I will ask if you could enjoy life, which would be preserved by the constant execution of so many human beings—your countrymen, your former friends, and almost your worshippers. The pangs of such a situation will be made more acute, by reflecting on the hallowed motive of many of those who would aim their daggers at your bosom. That, like the last of the Romans, they would strike, not from hatred to the man, but love to the country.

From a knowledge of your own disposition, and present feelings, your Excellency will not be willing to believe, that you could ever be brought to commit an act of tyranny, or even to execute justice with unnecessary rigor. But trust me, sir, that there is nothing more corrupting, nothing more destructive of the noblest and finest feelings of our nature, than the exercise of unlimited power. The man who, in the beginning of such a career, might shudder at the idea of taking away the life of a fellow-being, might soon have his conscience so seared by the repetition of crime, that the agonies of his murdered victims might become music to his soul, and the drippings of his scaffold afford "blood enough to swim in." History is full of such examples.

From this disgusting picture, permit me to call the attention of your Excellency to one of a different character. It exhibits you as the constitutional Chief Magistrate of a free people. Giving to their representatives the influence of your great name and talents, to reform the abuses which, in a long reign of tyranny and misrule, have fastened upon every branch of the administration. The army, and its swarm of officers, reduced within the limits of real usefulness, placed on the frontiers, and no longer permitted to control public opinion, and be the terror of the peaceful citizen. Br the removal of this incubus from the treasury, and the establishment of order, responsibility, and economy, in the expenditures of the government, it would soon be enabled to dispense with the odious monopolies, and the duty of the *Alcavala*, which have operated with so malign an effect upon commerce and agriculture, and, indeed, upon the revenues which they were intended to augment. No longer oppressed by these shackles, industry would everywhere revive: the farmer and the artisan, cheered by the prospect of ample reward for their labor, would redouble their exertions: foreigners, with their capital and skill in the arts, would crowd hither, to enjoy the advantages which could scarcely, elsewhere, be found: and Colombia would soon exhibit the reality of the beautiful fiction of Fenelon—Salentum rising from misery and oppression, to prosperity and happiness, under the councils and direction of the concealed goddess.

What objections can be urged against this course? Can any one, acquainted with the circumstances of the country, doubt its success, in restoring and maintaining tranquillity? The people would certainly not revolt against themselves; and none of the chiefs who are supposed to be factiously inclined, would think of opposing the strength of the nation, when directed by your talents and authority. But it is said, that the want of intelligence amongst the people unfits them for the government. Is it not right, however, that the experiment should be fairly tried? I have already said, that this has not been done. For myself, I do not hesitate to declare my firm belief, that it will succeed. The people of Colombia possess many traits, suitable for a republican government. A more orderly, forbearing, and well-disposed people are nowhere to be met with. Indeed, it may safely be asserted, that their faults and vices are attributable to the cursed government to which they have been so long subjected, and to the intolerant character of the religion, whilst their virtues are all their own. But, admitting their present want of intelligence, no one has ever doubted their capacity to acquire knowledge, and under the strong motives which exist, to obtain it, supported by the influence of your Excellency, it would soon be obtained.

To yourself, the advantage would be as great as to the country; like acts of mercy, the blessings would be reciprocal; your personal happiness secured, and your fame elevated to a height which would leave but a single competition in the estimation of posterity. In bestowing the palm of merit, the world has become wiser than formerly. The successful warrior is no longer regarded as entitled to the first place in the temple of fame. Talents of this kind have become too common, and too often used for mischievous purposes, to be regarded as they once were. In this enlightened age, the mere hero of the field, and the successful leader of armies, may, for the moment, attract attention. But it will be such as is bestowed upon the passing meteor, whose blaze is no longer remembered, when it is no longer seen. To be esteemed eminently great, it is necessary to be eminently good. The qualities of the hero and the general must be devoted to the advantage of mankind, before he will be permitted to assume the title of their benefactor; and the station which he will hold in their regard and affections will depend, not upon the number and the splendor of his victories, but upon the results and the use he may make of the influence he acquires from them.

If the fame of our Washington depended upon his military achievements, would the common consent of the world allow him the pre-eminence he possesses? The victories at Trenton, Monmouth, and York, brilliant as they were, exhibiting, as they certainly did, the highest grade of military talents, are scarcely thought of. The source of the veneration and esteem which is entertained for his character, by every description of politicians—the monarchist and aristocrat, as well as the republican, is to be found in his undeviating and exclusive devotedness to the interest of his country. No selfish consideration was ever suffered to intrude itself into his mind. For his country he conquered; and the unrivalled and increasing prosperity of that country is constantly adding fresh glory to his name. General; the course which he pursued is open to you, and it depends upon yourself to attain the eminence which he has reached before you.

To the eyes of military men, the laurels you won on the fields of Vargas, Bayaca, and Carebobo, will be forever green; but will that content you? Are you willing that your name should descend to posterity, amongst the mass of those whose fame has been derived from shedding human blood, without a single advantage to the human race? Or, shall it be united to that of Washington, as the founder and the father of a great and happy people? The choice is before you. The friends of liberty throughout the world, and the people of the United States in particular, are waiting your decision with intense anxiety. Alexander toiled and conquered to attain the applause of the Athenians; will you regard as nothing the opinions of a nation which has evinced its superiority over that celebrated people, in the science most useful to man, by having carried into actual practice a system of government, of which the wisest Athenians had but a glimpse in theory, and considered as a blessing never to be realized, however ardently to be desired? The place which you are to occupy m their esteem depends upon yourself. Farewell.

W. H. HARRISON.

Extracts from the address delivered before the Hamilton County Agricultural Society by General Harrison, June 16, 1831.

"The encouragement of agriculture, gentlemen, would be praiseworthy in any country; in our own it is peculiarly so. Not only to multiply the means and enjoyment of life, but as giving greater stability and security to our political institutions. In all ages and in au countries. It has been observed, that the cultivators of the soil, are those who are least willing to part with their rights, and submit themselves to the will of a master. I have no doubt also, that a taste for agricultural pursuits, is the best means of disciplining the ambition of those daring spirits, who occasionally spring up in the world, for good or for evil, to defend or destroy the liberties of their fellow-men, as the principles received from education or circumstances may tend. As long as the leaders of the Roman armies were taken from the plough, to the plough they were willing to return. Never in the character of General, forgetting the duties of the citizen, and ever ready to exchange the sword and the triumphal purple, for the homely vestments of the husbandman.

The history of this far-famed republic is full of instances of this kind; but none more remarkable than our own age and country have produced. The fascinations of power and the trappings of command, were as much despised, and the enjoyment of rural scenes, and rural employments as highly prized by our Washington, as by Cincinnatus or Regulus. At the close of his glorious military career, he says, 'I am preparing to return to that domestic retirement which it is well known I left with the deepest regret, and for which I have not ceased to sigh through a long and painful absence.

Your efforts, gentlemen, to diffuse a taste for agriculture amongst men of all descriptions and professions, may produce results more important even than increasing the means of subsistence, and the enjoyment of life. It may cause some future conqueror for his country, to end his career

"Guiltless of his country's blood."

* * *

To the heart cheering prospect of flocks and herds feeding on unrivalled pastures, fields of grain, exhibiting the scriptural proof that the seed had been cast on good ground—how often is the eye of the philanthropic traveller disgusted with the dark, unsightly manufactories of a certain poison—poison to the body and the soul. A modem Æneas or Ulyssses might mistake them for entrances into the Infernal Regions; nor would they greatly err. But unlike those passages which conducted the Grecian and Trojan heroes on their pious errands, the scenes to which these conduct the unhappy wretch who shall enter them are those, exclusively, of misery and woe. No relief to the sad picture; no Tartarus *there*, no Elysium *here*. It is all Tartarian darkness, and not unfrequently Tartarian crime. I speak more freely of the practice of converting the material of the "staff of life" (and for which so many human beings yearly perish) into an article which is so destructive of health and happiness, because in that way I have sinned myself; *but in that way I shall sin no more."*—See page 134.

GENERAL HARRISON TO HON. HARMAR DENNY.

NORTH BEND, Dec. 2, 1838.

DEAR SIR,

As it is probable that you have by this time returned to Pittsburgh, I do myself the honor to acknowledge the receipt of your letter from Philadelphia, containing the proceedings of the National Democratic Anti-masonic Convention, which lately convened in that city. With feelings of the deepest gratitude, I read the resolution unanimously adopted, nominating me as a candidate for the President of the United States. This is the second time that I have received from that patriotic party, of which you yourself are a distinguished member, the highest evidence of confidence that can be given to a citizen of our republic. I would attempt to describe my sense of the obligations I owe them, if I were not convinced that any language which I could command would fall far short of what I really feel. If, however, the wishes of the convention should be realized, and if I should second their efforts, I shall have it in my power to manifest my gratitude in a manner more acceptable to those whom you represent, than by any professions of it which I could at this time make; I mean by exerting my utmost efforts to carry out the principles set forth in their resolutions, by arresting the progress of the measures "destructive to the prosperity of the people, and tending to the subversion of their liberties," and substituting for them those sound democratic republican doctrines, upon which the administration of Jefferson and Madison were conducted.

Among the principles proper to be adopted by any executive sincerely desirous to restore the administration to its original simplicity and purity, I deem the following to be of prominent importance.

I. To confine his service to a single term.

II. To disclaim all right of control over the public treasure, with the exception of such part of it as may be appropriated by law, to carry on the public services, and that to be applied precisely as the law may direct, and drawn from the treasury agreeably to the long established forms of that department.

III. That he should never attempt to influence the elections, either by the people or the state legislatures, nor suffer the federal officers under his control to take any other part in them than by giving their own votes when they possess the right of voting.

IV. That in the exercise of the veto power, he should limit his rejection of bills to, 1st, Such as are, in his opinion, unconstitutional; 2d, Such as tend to encroach on the rights of the states or individuals; 3d, Such as involving deep interests, may, in his opinion, require more mature deliberation or reference to the will of the people, to be ascertained at the succeeding elections.

V. That be should never suffer the influence of his office to be used for purposes of a purely party character.

VI. That in removals from office of those who hold their appointments during the pleasure of the Executive, the cause of such removal should be stated if requested, to the Senate, at the time the nomination of a successor if made.

And last, but not least in importance,

VII. That he should not suffer the executive department of the government to become the source of legislation: but leave the whole business of making laws for the Union to the department to which the Constitution has exclusively assigned it, until they have assumed that perfected shape, where and when alone the opinions of the Executive may be heard."

The question may perhaps be asked of me, what security I have in my power to offer, if the majority of the American people should select me for their chief magistrate, that I would adopt the principles which I have herein laid down as those upon which my administration would be conducted; I could only answer, by referring to my conduct, and the disposition manifested in the discharge of the duties of several important offices, which have heretofore been conferred upon me. If the power placed in my hands has, on even a single occasion, been used for any purpose other than that for which it was given, or retained longer than was necessary to accomplish the objects designated by those from whom the trusts were received, I will acknowledge that either will constitute a sufficient reason for discrediting any promise I may make, under the circumstances in which I am now placed.

I am, dear sir, truly yours,
W. H. HARRISON.

To the Hon. Harmar Denny.

GENERAL HARRISON TO THE EDITOR OF THE OHIO CONFEDERATE.

NORTH BEND, Oct. 18, 1839.

DEAR SIR,—The article you wrote in reply to some abusive remarks made upon me by the editors of two of the Ohio newspapers, is still going the rounds of publication in the journals of the Atlantic cities. It is at least once a week brought to my notice, and yet I have delayed to execute the intention I formed when I first saw it, to express in a letter to you, my deep sense of gratitude for the exalted terms in which you have been pleased to speak of me, and my admiration of the generosity and nobleness of soul which prompted yon to become my defender, under the circumstances in which you stand in relation to those by whom I was assailed. I can give no other reason for the delay than the apprehension that I should not be able properly to express my feelings on an occasion where they had been so strongly excited. They are, I trust, such as they ought to be, and such as a heart like yours will readily believe to exist in the bosom of another who owes a debt of gratitude that he despairs of ever being able to repay. But, however, highly I may value the approbation, coming from a source the purity of which no one can doubt, candor obliges me to say that you have done me more than justice, in attributing to me uncommon merit in my disinterested management of the public funds submitted to my control, and in the execution of the important powers with which I have been clothed, at different times, by the Government of the United States.

As it regards the first, how could I act otherwise, considering the tutorage I received in my youth, and which is common to all brought up in the part of the country from which we both came? There were circumstances in my situation, too, which would have rendered the guilt of any dereliction of duty in me of deeper dye than in most of the other public officers. I allude to the great confidence (manifested by the extraordinary powers conferred upon me) reposed in me by the great statesmen and patriots under whom it was my good fortune to act. Take a sample or two; I was Governor of Indiana, (at that time it comprised what is now Indiana, Illinois, Michigan, and Wisconsin,) ex-officio Superintendent of Indian Affairs, and by the Constitution (the ordinance) vested with the power to appoint all the officers (under the first grade,) and to lay off counties and fix seats of justice. Under the second, a complete control over the Legislature. I was, moreover, vested by Congress with the complete control over the public domain at Vincennes, and in the Illinois country, for the settlement of all the claims to land made by the "French and British governments, or by courts or commandants *claiming* the rights to make such grants, the whole of the land so granted, or as much thereof as might appear to me to be reasonable and just." With these great powers in my hand, President Jefferson, in 1804, sent me a commission constituting me sole commissioner for treating with all the northwestern tribes, with the power to draw for any money I might think necessary for the accomplishment of the objects committed to me. My compensation was fixed at $6 per diem and my expenses, when I was acting as commissioner, but I was entirely left to myself to determine when I should be considered as acting under this commission, or the ordinary one of superintendent. I have no means near me of ascertaining the whole amount of compensation I charged for the thirteen treaties I negotiated, ill the course of the eleven years that I acted under the commission; I am persuaded however, that it did not exceed $4,000—at most $5,000.

As soon as Louisiana was acquired, I was made by a law of Congress, (at the suggestion of Mr. Jefferson,) ex-officio Governor of "Upper Louisiana." I do not positively know, his motive for this singular arrangement. But I do know, that he had it much at heart to convince the inhabitants of the newly acquired territory of the great difference between our Government and the corrupt one they had so long suffered under. Under this impression, I declined receiving the fee to which I was entitled by law, although those for Indian licenses would have brought me two or three thousand dollars, and refused to purchase any property, although I was tempted by the proprietor (A. Choteau) of three fourths of St. Louis and all the adjoining lands, with an individual moiety for assisting him to build up the town.

In the war of 1811, and that which commenced in 1812, I received almost a carte blanche as to appointments, organization of the army, expenditures, &c. Was it possible for me to bring dishonor upon the administration of these distinguished men, by using their unlimited confidence for any other purpose than that for which it was given?

"I have only room to add that I am, most truly, yours.

WILLIAM H. HARRISON.

Mr. MILDER, Editor of the Ohio Confederate."

THE OPINION OF A FOREIGNER.—M. Chevalier having encountered General Harrison at Cincinnati, in one of his letters, the following comment:—

"I had observed at the hotel table a man about the medium height, stout and muscular, and about the age of sixty years, yet with the active step and lively air of youth. I had been struck with his open and cheerful expression, the amenity of his open and certain air of command, which appeared through his plain dress. "That is" said my friend, "General Harrison, Clerk of the Cincinnati Court of Common Pleas."—"What! General Harrison of the Tippecanoe and the Thames?" "The same; the ex-general, the conqueror of Tecumseh and Proctor; the avenger of our disasters on the Raisin and Detroit; the ex-governor of the Territory of Indiana, the ex-senator in Congress, the ex-minister of the United States to one of the South American Republics. He has grown old in the service of his country, he has passed twenty years of his life in those fierce wars with the Indians in which there is less glory to be won, but more dangers to be encountered than at Tivoli and Austerlitz. He is now poor, with a numerous family, neglected by the Federal Government, although yet vigorous, because he had the independence to think for himself. As the opposition is in the majority here, his friends have bethought themselves of coming to his relief by removing the Clerk of Common Pleas, who was a Jackson man, and giving him the place, which is a lucrative one, as a sort of retiring pension. His friends in the East talk of making him President of the United States—meanwhile we have made him clerk of an inferior court."

www.ingramcontent.com/pod-product-compliance
Lightning Source LLC
Chambersburg PA
CBHW020423010526
44118CB00010B/398